MAJORCAN FOOD

With well over 3 million visitors ~~~~~ ~~ Majorca from Britain
alone, it is surprising that this is the first book in English on
Majorcan food and cookery.

The wealth of recipes which the author describes, and which
she sets in their historical and geographical contexts, show that
there is a great variety in Majorcan cooking which makes the
most of the fresh produce found in and around the island and
beautifully displayed every day of the week in village markets.

ELIZABETH CARTER first went to Majorca in 1981, under
the compulsion of an urge to live in another country, speak its
language and enter its culture.

The island turned out to be the right choice, for she loved it,
especially the quiet villages of the interior, away from the tracks
beaten by tourists. It was there, and in small fishing villages, that
she learned about Majorcan food and cookery of the traditional
kind, study of which has been her main hobby ever since.

Elizabeth Carter, who has a degree from Manchester Poly-
technic in Art and Design worked in advertising for a while, and
ran her own restaurant in London for nearly five years, besides
putting in a stint as a professional restaurant inspector and critic.
She lives in Hackney, travels frequently all over the UK, and
goes to Majorca whenever she can and for as long as she can.

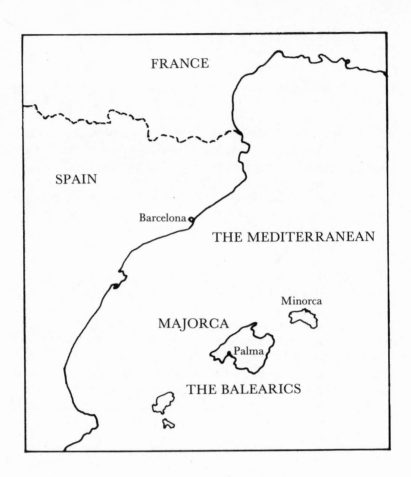

Majorcan Food and Cookery

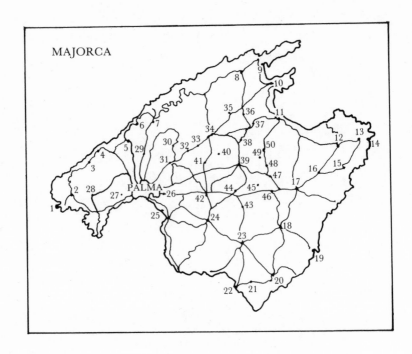

MAJORCA

1. Puerto de Andraitx
2. Andraitx
3. Estellenchs
4. Banyalbufar
5. Valldemosa
6. Deya
7. Soller
8. Pollensa
9. Puerto de Pollensa
10. Alcudia
11. Can Picafort
12. Artá
13. Capdepera
14. Cala Rajada
15. Son Servera
16. Sant Llorenc
17. Manacor
18. Felanitx
19. Porto Colom
20. Santanyi
21. Ses Salines
22. Colonia de Sant Jordi
23. Campos
24. Llucmajor
25. Can Pastilla
26. Son Ferriol
27. Genova
28. Calviá
29. Bunyola
30. Alaró
31. Santa Maria
32. Consell
33. Binisalem
34. Inca
35. Campanet
36. La Puebla
37. Muró
38. Llubi
39. Sineu
40. Costitx
41. Sencellas
42. Algaida
43. Porreras
44. Montuiri
45. Sant Joan
46. Villafranca
47. Petra
48. Ariany
49. Maria de la Salud
50. Santa Margarita

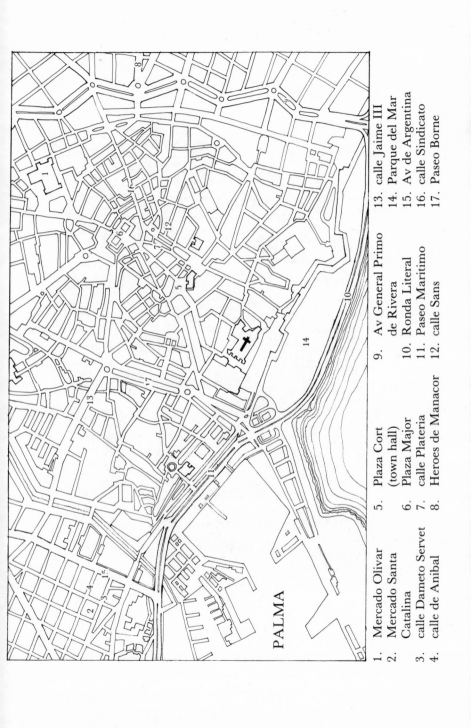

PALMA

1. Mercado Olivar
2. Mercado Santa
   Catalina
3. calle Dameto Servet
4. calle de Anibal

5. Plaza Cort
   (town hall)
6. Plaza Major
7. calle Plateria
8. Heroes de Manacor

9. Av General Primo
   de Rivera
10. Ronda Literal
11. Paseo Maritimo
12. calle Sans

13. calle Jaime III
14. Parque del Mar
15. Av de Argentina
16. calle Sindicato
17. Paseo Borne

Majorcan Food and Cookery

by
Elizabeth Carter

PROSPECT BOOKS

1989

For their honeymoon they went to the Balearic Islands. The exquisite loveliness of Mallorca, its gentle airs and mild winter suns, its great sweet oranges, little deep-streeted Moorish towns, ancient inns and blue bays, its olive-grown mountains, straying, jingling goats and beautiful and amiable inhabitants, combined with the excessive love which this couple bore one another to make the weeks they spent on this island a period of complete and unmarred bliss, culminating in an exquisite and smiling Christmas in the little orange-gardened town of Soller.

Rose Macaulay, *Crewe Train*

British Library Cataloguing in Publication Data
Carter, Elizabeth
  Majorcan food and cookery.
  1. Majorca. Food. Drinks. Food & drinks
  I. Title
  641'.0946'754

ISBN 0-907325-43-2

The drawings in this book are by Anna MacMiadhacháin, except for those on pp 53 and 71 and the maps, which are by Soun Vannithone; the drawings of invertebrate marine creatures, which come from *Mediterranean Seafood* by Alan Davidson; and the drawings of fish which are taken by kind permission from the FAO *Species Identification Sheets for the Mediterranean and the Black Sea* (volume II, Vertebrates), Rome 1987. © the artists and sources indicated.

© cover design by Corinna Sargood 1989

Published by Prospect Books, 45 Lamont Road, London SW10 0HU

Printed and bound by Smith Settle, Otley, West Yorkshire

Contents

Foreword

Here, to borrow a horticultural phrase, is a book which has grown organically. Cookery books of this description are not common. When they do occur, they are usually one-off affairs; the work of people who are not professional authors; the fruit of a decade or more of real experience (as opposed to six months of 'research'); fuelled by enthusiasm rather than cupidity; and written in an engagingly fresh and modest way.

This is the kind of book I like; and it has been my privilege to be the publisher of several such, usually dealing with cookery in just one small part of the world, but dealing with it thoroughly.

Elizabeth Carter's book falls squarely into this category, and is the first in English to deal with Majorcan cookery. What a blessing it is that she treats the subject seriously (although not solemnly), and that she writes about it 'from inside', being thoroughly familiar with Majorcan markets and kitchens! This familiarity shines through the pages of the book, and assures us that we are reading about the realities, which in a place like Majorca can only too easily be invisible to and untasted by the tides of tourists flowing in and out.

The realities can also be obscured by the misleading notion that Majorcan cookery is merely a minor variation of the Catalan cuisine.

Catalan cuisine was of great importance in the Middle Ages; indeed it ranked among the most important in Europe. Nowadays, it falls into place as a regional cuisine of great interest but limited importance; centred on Barcelona and exhibiting variations throughout Catalonia. But Catalonia is on the Spanish mainland. The fact that the people of Majorca (and Minorca) speak a Catalan dialect does not mean their cookery is simply a dialect form of Catalan cookery. To be sure, there are connections, often close, but the true Majorcan cookery, found in Majorcan homes and revealed to us in this book, stands up as something in its own right, such as one would expect to find in an island, and especially in an island so beautiful and fertile.

When George Sand and Chopin made their escapade to Majorca, they took their problems with them and found new problems there. George Sand dipped her pen in vinegar to describe these. But the acidity of her description, so powerful that it may, as one commentator supposes, have delayed the arrival of tourism in the island for over half a century, reminds us that until recent times Majorca was a truly remote place, largely insulated from the world, and that when we acquaint our-selves, under Elizabeth Carter's guidance, with true Majorcan cookery we are encountering something which, like her book, has been of organic growth and is of absorbing interest.

Alan Davidson
April 1989

George Sand,
adapted from
a picture by
Maurice Sand

Introduction

It was at one of the regular family gatherings that I finally met Baltazar's parents. On Christmas eve, it is traditional for families to congregate after midnight Mass to drink thick hot chocolate into which *ensaimadas* (sweet pastries) are dipped.

At this point I had met most of his huge Catholic family for they ran many of the commercial concerns in the little fishing port, Puerto de Andraitx, where he lived. But I had not met his parents. Meeting parents is a serious matter. In some of the old Majorcan communities, an occasion when, in many eyes, one becomes 'novia official', in other words engaged. In such a small place, it was a wonder that we had not bumped into each other and, indeed, for the last few months his mother had been going round the port making enquiries about me and leaving strong hints, gleefully passed on, that she would like to meet me.

Christmas approached and his mother sent a message inviting me to meet them after midnight Mass. I arrived, nervous, to a house full of Baltazar's relatives. We had missed Mass because that year it was held at ten thirty; the priest wanted to go on later to a big village party that had been organised in a local restaurant.

Baltazar's mother, a direct woman, immediately asked my age, commenting that the age gap between him and me was exactly the same as that between her daughter and her husband. Then she offered to show me around the house. We finished in a spare bedroom, furnished in traditional Mallorquin manner with large, dark ornate furniture. She opened a huge chest and pulled out a splendid crocheted bedspread. 'I made this for my grandson, when he marries, and this' — out came another — 'for the other grandson'. Then she brought out a third in blue and white. 'This is for Baltazar when he marries. ?Te gusta? [Do you like it?]' I politely murmered yes. 'Well, in that case, you'll have to marry him to get it' she finished triumphantly. I had obviously passed some sort of test.

Over the next couple of years when I lived in Majorca, she made it quite clear that she wished I would marry him, upping the stakes considerably from just a bedspread. It was not to be, but I remember her and her husband with great affection. They were kind to me and welcomed me into their family as if I were a daughter-in-law. It was through them that I learnt much about Majorcan food.

*   *   *   *   *

I first arrived in Majorca, speaking no Spanish, but seizing a rare opportunity to live in a foreign country and learn about its food and culture. Washing up in a restaurant seemed to me to be the best way to supplement my Spanish lessons and learn something of the local food. At the same time, I started to write a weekly food column for the English-language *Majorca Daily Bulletin*. Amongst the requests for good scone recipes were an increasing number of pleas for more information on local food and cooking. This started off my research into things Majorcan, a process which was to take several years.

Majorca is the largest of the Balearic islands, similar in scale to Cornwall. Its ancient churches, monasteries, medieval villages, great country houses and gardens are set in a scenery of immense diversity. On the one hand, two mountain ranges sweep across the island, reaching as high as 5000 ft on the north west side. On their terraced lower reaches, gnarled olive trees in groves grey and dusty contrast with the deep colour of the lemon and orange trees. On the other hand, between the two ranges, is a wide beautiful plain of intensely cultivated land, Es Pla. Here the almonds for which Majorca is famous grow, as well as apricots, figs, peaches and plums, melons, tomatoes, potatoes, the prized pimentos and aubergines, along with vines for the developing wine industry.

Until the onset of tourism, agricultural land was highly valued and inherited only by sons. Daughters were left the seemingly worthless land that made up Majorca's 186 miles of coast; a coastline punctuated and indented by coves, wide-sweeping sandy bays and spectacular rocky headlands with magnificent drops to the water below. Majorca's proximity to the west and north of Europe made inevitable the development of this beautiful coastline for tourism which in its turn made Majorcan women very rich. Their erstwhile worthless coastal inheritance soared in value — under Spanish law women retain all property rights on marriage.

Tourism is still confined mainly to the coast: the inland towns, villages and surrounding countryside have hardly been affected, although the whole island has greatly profited from the wealth brought by it. Previously poverty and primitive conditions were common. The English writer, Robert Graves, who first settled on the island in the 1930s describes the living conditions in the village of Deya then: 'In 1934 I bought the guest-house that had belonged to the former squires of Deya ... of the eight rooms only two bedrooms were glazed. Several of the cottages of the village had no glass at all, and the old women used to sit spinning on their thresholds in all weathers.'

Twenty years later the situation was remarkably similar. A Majorcan friend, Madó, described to me the fishing village of Puerto de Andraitx, now highly developed with up-market villas and a yacht marina, as it appeared to her in the early 1950s. Madó's parents had fled the island in 1936 at the outbreak of the Civil War and had settled in Marseilles where Madó was brought up and educated. She returned to Puerto de Andraitx to marry Baltazar's elder brother and moved with him into a house overlooking the fishermen's quay. In her Castilian Spanish, heavily accented with French, she said that she will never understand how she coped. Used to the bustle of Marseilles and mid-20th century comforts, she found herself in a small village with no electricity or gas, water drawn from a well and all cooking done over a wood-fired stove. Roads were dirt tracks and the men customarily gathered in the bar in the evenings while the women stayed at home.

Prosperity has changed all this and now Majorcans enjoy one of the highest per capita incomes in Spain, but they still retain a strong sense of identity. Although enjoying late 20th century comforts in the apartments and villas that are their main residences, they still appreciate the old ways. Madó, for

11

instance, inherited from her grandmother a small country cottage. Now she likes to keep it in its original state by choice, using it as a weekend retreat or for entertaining family and friends on fine Sundays in the winter. They cook on an open wood fire outside the front door under the covered porch — although she cheats by allowing herself the luxury of a butane gas stove for use in summer.

Many Majorcan families own such *casitas,* often simple one-room huts, which used to be inhabited by the shepherds. They escape to them in summer travelling from the dry, dusty heat of the towns. On winter weekends the entire family, aunts, uncles, in-laws included, gather for large country picnics. The outside fire is stoked up and all manner of Majorcan sausages grilled together with thick slices of pork, lamb chops and freshly-gathered wild mushrooms; all eaten with great chunks of fresh bread and young Majorcan red wine.

One New Year's Day I was invited to lunch by a branch of Baltazar's family living in Andraitx village, several miles from the fishing port. Twenty-four members of the family were gathered. In the central patio, common to all these village houses, various sons-in-law were tending to the cooking of the first course, an immense *arroz brut* (see p 68), based on rice, game and wild mushrooms. Instead of the wood-fired stove, they were using a huge gas ring set on a tripod over the butane gas bottle and cooking the food in an enormous metal paella. At these extended family gatherings everyone helps with the cooking. But it is still the women who have to wash up.

It is in the home that variety can be found. In spring, a stew from tender young broad beans, sprigs of mint and the Majorcan spiced blood sausage, *butifarron,* can be made in an earthenware dish; or you could have wild asparagus cooked in an omelette of new-laid eggs; or a casserole of Majorcan lamb containing a choice of seasonal fruits and vegetables and subtly spiced with cinnamon.

In summer, a dish of large sweet red tomatoes bought from a country town market stall requires only salt and olive oil to make an exquisite salad; a lunch of sea bream, bright-eyed with freshness, baked whole in the oven with potatoes, lemons and olive oil is delicious, especially when rounded off with fruit. Especially good at this time of year are sweet melons from Villafranca (where every September they celebrate their *fiesta de melones*); sun-warmed figs, their insides thickly-jammy, and rich plump grapes.

In winter, snails gathered at night after a fall of rain are cooked with aromatic herbs to which vegetables, chopped almonds and the Majorcan sausage, *sobrasada,* are added. For special occasions, like Christmas, a moist almond cake is often served with Majorca's famous almond ice cream or a sweet filled *ensaimada* of giant proportions bought from the local baker (see p 119).

Basically, Majorcan dishes are derived from peasant cooking and are domestic in origin. There is no 'haute cuisine'. A criticism levelled at Spanish cooking in general is that its presentation is poor. Colman Andrews in his book *Catalan Cuisine* labels it as 'The Brown Food Problem'. This is not how I saw it in Majorca. Certainly food is regarded as something to be eaten and enjoyed with little attention to its looks. But fresh fish baked with peppers, lemons and black olives, hearty soups of vegetables, meat and pulses, saffron- and paprika-coloured rice dishes have a strong, immediately colourful impact.

Majorcans shop for fresh meat and vegetables daily. If you visit a supermarket, you find a limited selection of frozen and convenience foods — I once counted only 7 frozen prepared dishes at the largest supermarket on the island. They also use a wide variety of ingredients. It is not unusual to be stuck behind a woman in a butcher's buying a quarter of a chicken, 1 pigs trotter, 1 *butifarron,* 1 piece of pork, a few pieces of ham bone and some mince (minced to order) all for lunch that day. Vegetables and fruit are bought in profusion and prepared straightaway. Food is never stewed for hours, a method that usually results in an overall brown colour.

Perhaps most casual visitors to Majorca would expect to be presented with food very much like that served on the nearby Spanish mainland. Although geographically, ethnically and linguistically, Majorca is considered part of the 'Catalan lands' and the cooking reflects this, there are obvious differences.

Climate and produce are logical explanations for the similarities in their cuisines. Yet Catalan cooking is one of the oldest and most respected culinary styles in Spain and is more sophisticated.

Majorcan food in comparison is more down-to-earth and peasant in style. Two typical regional desserts show up the difference. *Crema Catalana* (not unlike *crème brulée*) requires some skill in the making. It is smooth-textured and delicately flavoured. *Pudin,* the Majorcan dessert, is solid and filling. Stale *ensaimadas,* milk, eggs, caramel and cinnamon are roughly baked to form a firm bread pudding, eaten cold in thick slices. Even the names show up the disparity.

An explanation for the similarities between the two culinary styles comes from the time when both areas were dominated by the Moors. Even today, more than 700 years since the Islamic rule ended, its heritage is still discernible. Both Catalan and Mallorquin (the Catalan dialect of Majorca) are liberally sprinkled with Arabic words. Many Majorcan place names such as Almudaina, Atalaya, Valldemosa and Binisalem are of Moorish origin.

*   *   *   *   *

Let me briefly outline the history of the island, since this will make clear the influences involved in the evolution of the people and their food.

Until the Middle Ages, the Balearic Islands tended to be occupied by whichever power dominated the Mediterranean. There are still remains of prehistoric peoples, and of the Greeks and the Rhodians, but the men of the Balearics entered the pages of written history because of one particular skill: they were experts with the sling and were trained in its use from an early age. It is said that parents would place food high in a tree and their son would have to dislodge it with stones from his sling before he could eat. When the Carthaginians occupied the islands they recruited these Balearic slingers into their armies during the long war against the rising powers of Rome in the third century BC. Most of their battles began with lethal showers of stones from Balearic slings.

Later the islanders appeared to have turned to piracy, for in 123 BC, a Roman force landed in Majorca to suppress the piratical activities of the inhabitants. Roman colonies were established at Palma and Pollensa. During the next few centuries Romans who fell foul of the emperors were often exiled to Majorca.

After the fall of the Roman empire, the Vandals took over Majorca in 465 AD until they, in turn, were thrown out by a Byzantine army under Belisarius. Then, in 902 AD, the Moors arrived and, in the course of their occupation, piracy, based on Palma, proved once again to be a 'nice little earner'.

The Moors were driven out by King Jaime of Aragon (1213-1276), who invaded Majorca in 1229 and managed to add the island to his kingdom. At his death in 1276, his lands were divided between his two sons, Pedro III of Aragon and Jaime II of Mallorca. The island stayed an independent kingdom until 1343 when Pedro IV reunited it with the kingdom of Aragon, which included the Catalan area. It has remained joined to Spain ever since.

The next four centuries saw the Mediterranean plagued by pirates based in North Africa. Majorca suffered many raids and eventually provided itself with a chain of coastal watch towers (*atalayas*) to give warning of the approach of raiders. Many of these towers still exist.

The Italian Fascists based themselves in Majorca during the Spanish Civil War and did little to endear themselves to the local population.

During the Franco years, attempts to suppress the Catalan, Galician and Basque languages were made. Efforts to make Castilian the official language have resulted, since the coming of democracy, in an increased desire for a regional identity. In Majorca this can be seen in the new awareness of the Mallorquin language and things Mallorquin.

*   *   *   *   *

Part of this awareness can be seen in the development of restaurants on the island.

Quite simply, there were no restaurants until tourism began. In 1809 there was one good inn in Palma which Sir John Carr,

15

in his *Descriptive Travels in the Southern and Eastern Parts of Spain and the Balearic Islands* (1811), describes with great delight the breakfast of chocolate and cakes, followed by a 'dinner admirably dressed of soup, meat, fowls and generally two dishes of game, either rabbit, hare, quails, partridges, thrushes or snipe, with which the island abounds, pastry, aboundance of the best wine, a dessert of the finest fruits, coffee'. He added that the supper was nearly as plentiful as the dinner. The inn was managed by a Frenchman.

By 1888 things had declined. Charles W. Wood wrote in *Letters from Majorca:* 'It cannot be denied that if Palma had a large and well-organised hotel, appointed more like the hotels one is generally accustomed to, its attractions would be increased, and more visitors would lighten it with their countenances.'

Even those cool atmospheric cellar restaurants dominated by massive oak wine casks in the town of Inca, which give such a strong impression of being old-established restaurants did not serve food until the end of the 1940s. Until then, they had been retail wine shops but would serve wine by the glass to people who brought their own food to eat on the premises.

Hotels, when they opened, served an internationally-based cuisine to an international clientele. The food is either immaculately presented and expensive, or fast foods like egg and chips or hamburgers and aimed at the tourist. It is interesting to note that when McDonalds opened their first branch on Majorca, it was based in a major tourist resort popular with British tourists, not in the island's capital, Palma.

Away from tourist areas, a different kind of restaurant has been springing up and rapidly growing in popularity. These offer *la cocina mallorquina,* but can be disappointing. The food is not poor quality, but foreigners tend to wonder where the fresh vegetables are and, since most restaurants seem to offer identical menus, why the choice is so limited. The standard fish soup, paella, meat and fish *a la plancha* appear monotonously, yet fresh vegetables and an enormous range of fish can be seen in the markets in their seasonal profusion ready to provide ever-changing dishes.

Majorcans think that restaurants are for social gatherings,

and the food is not expected to be as varied as that cooked at home. This does not help the visitor. Nor does the fact that it is comparatively rare to be invited to a Majorcan home for a formal meal.

In recent years the Majorcan restaurant association, *Associació Empresarial de Restauració de Mallorca,* has worked hard to promote local food in local restaurants and every May it organises an exhibition of Majorcan cooking for the public in the Borne in central Palma. Held in a long marquee, *La Mostra de Cuina Mallorquina* is great fun to attend. Participating restaurants from all over the island each offer one dish for tasting, either adapted from an old recipe or a new idea using local produce. They are backed up by stalls representing the major wine producers, fruit growers and some of the best bakers and ice cream makers on the island.

So, for a small sum, visitors to the exhibition can sample such dishes as rabbit with almond sauce, quails with meatballs, *frito mallorquin,* washed down with the different Majorcan wines, and the island's olives, capers, dried fruits, local pastries and ice creams, the whole experience ending with a strong cup of coffee and some of the local liqueurs. It's crowded, lively and has the air of a fiesta, and one can learn a lot about the food and the people. Majorcans take their food very seriously and love to discuss it. I've witnessed some really heated arguments about what vegetables to cook with snails and in which village the best *greixonera de brossat* is made.

This strong awareness of a Mallorquin culinary identity bodes well for the future. But it is not entirely new.

In 1961, *La Cocina Selecta Mallorquina,* a most unusual cookery book, was published in Majorca. The author, Coloma Abrinas Vidal, affectionately known to all as Madó Coloma, could neither read nor write and dictated her recipes to a friend. She drew on her experiences as a domestic cook in service in the first half of this century, before improved communications and tourism opened the island to new ideas about food, and her book reveals the native cookery of times long ago.

Nestor Lujan, one of Spain's most eminent food writers, describes her recipe for *caracoles con sobrasada* as one of the best regional Spanish dishes he has ever come across. She refused to allow her book to be translated into any other language, nor would she let editors tamper with the style. The recipes are essentially for the experienced cook as few quantities or times are indicated; and they are interspersed with advice, prayers and riddles. When asked why her book was in Spanish rather than Mallorquin, Madó Coloma would reply that nobody could read Mallorquin any longer. (After the attempted suppression of the language during the Franco years Mallorquin survived only orally and adult Majorcans have had to make an effort to learn to read and write it again.) She died at Campos in March 1987, aged 98. At her death her book had run to 17 editions. Yet Madó Coloma was none too happy about her book being sold in book shops; she much preferred people to visit her at her home where she could chat and offer them her famous rice wine.

This ancient domestic culinary tradition can still be found. Away from the ribbon development of the coastal areas one is still able to glimpse the way of life that has endured for centuries. The agricultural scene and the layout of the towns remain almost unchanged since the Middle Ages. Villages and small towns still hold their weekly open air markets in the shadow of the parish church. Driving around, out of the summer high season, one can still come across a lone roadside stall selling the seasonal produce of the area or pull into a farm offering potatoes, beans, fruits and free range eggs. Eating Sunday lunch in a crowded Mallorquin country restaurant, one is surrounded by whole families, from the newest arrival to an infirm great-grandmother. Grouped around tables set for 20 or more, a now dying country custom is occasionally to be seen. All the men sit along one side of the table and all the women along the other.

*   *   *   *   *

I found Majorca a magical island; one of the island's most famous visitors, George Sand, could not deny this, however much she might have wanted to: 'In Majorca I could make no comparison with any remembered place. The people, the houses, the plants, the very pebbles on the road, had a distinct character of their own. My children were so struck by it that they collected everything, and wanted to fill our trunks with those beautiful blocks of quartz and veined marble which are built into the dry-stoned walls of every enclosure. Some of the peasants who saw us gathering even dead twigs mistook us for apothecaries; others for simple lunatics.'

Fortunately, I was given a far better reception than the misunderstood George Sand. I was lucky enough to meet Majorcans who introduced me not only to a different way of life, but also to the wonderful meals cooked in the home. They inspired this book. Please use it with the same spirit of adventure that I had when I first approached the island, its people and its cooking.

Acknowledgements

When writing this book, I received advice from many Mallorquins — friends and total strangers, who, on realising my genuine interest in Majorcan food, went out of their way to help. How can I list them all? The shop assistant in C'an Tia who painstakingly explained the method of making Majorcan sausages; Juan at Can Joan in Genova who taught me all I ever want to know about cleaning snails and tripe; Gaspar Alemany who supplied a typewriter in an emergency; the various members of the Vera family ... the list is endless: I thank them all.

Most especially, I would like to thank my parents for their long-suffering support and everyone at Prospect Books, namely, Alan and Jane Davidson and Kate Scarborough.

MARKETS

Majorcan women are fierce market shoppers; they don't queue but rely on force of character and strength of voice to be served quickly. Their usual bulky size is another asset. Once they have the full attention of the stall holder, eagle eyes ensure that no damaged or inferior goods are palmed off on them. The English sense of queuing and fair play has no place here, so if you want reasonably quick service, you must be forceful.

Of a number of permanent covered markets in Palma the MERCADO OLIVAR is the biggest and best — two floors packed with huge mounds of fruit, vegetables, fresh meat, hams, game, sausages, cheeses, dried fruits and nuts, dried beans and pulses. A separate section houses the fish, and an array of shellfish such as we would never see in Britain. There are mounds of delicately coloured rockfish, great slabs of swordfish, small sharks, fearsomely large rays, and silver heaps of tiny sardines. Stop for a second to examine something unusual and the fishmonger will exhort you loudly to buy. Heavily laden porters, lottery sellers and begging gypsies mingle with the crowds of determined shoppers.

The MERCADO SANTA CATALINA is a smaller version of this hectic, colourful medley, preferred by some for its easier-to-cope-with size. Both markets are open from 8 am to 2 pm every day except Sundays and fiestas and it is well worth while to look round these markets for the insight they give into the way of life of the Majorcans and the food they eat.

The Majorcan way of life is even more apparent at the weekly small town and village markets. Some have developed into major tourist attractions offering souvenirs, crafts ware, leather-goods and clothing as well as the seasonal local produce. Others, in tiny villages, consist of just a few stalls of market produce, hardware and clothing, but they are worth a visit because the villages are then seen at their liveliest. Some of the larger towns have permanent covered markets selling fish, meat, fruit and vegetables every day and their weekly market is just an extension of this, spilling out into the surrounding streets and offering a greater variety of food as well as clothing, leathergoods and household necessities.

INCA has the largest of the weekly markets, and this is the one most worth visiting; but, as tourists are coached in from all over the island, it is wise to arrive by 9 am in order to avoid the crowds. Pleasantly cool streets are neatly lined with stalls selling handbags, shoes, linen, pottery, hardware and electrical goods and lead into a square next to the permanent covered market. Here, in the big square, produce from the surrounding areas is for sale at remarkably low prices — all kinds of fruit and vege-tables, dried and fresh herbs, freshly-picked garden flowers dis-played in tin cans, bags of snails and free-range eggs. Some of the stalls are tiny, with just one or two items for sale, a pile of melons or some thinnings of lettuce or cauliflower leaves (the latter is delicious cooked like cabbage), or a heap of edible acorns. By 10.30 am the streets are almost impassable, full of both tourists and local people.

The one market on the island that has retained a strong medieval character is at SINEU, which is off the beaten track for most tourists and certainly for coach tours. Clustered round the impressive church, local farmers sell their produce at their stalls, whilst earthenware casseroles, cheap cotton dresses and aston-ishingly old-fashioned underwear are displayed on the ground. A few stalls to attract tourists have appeared, especially those of the gypsies with their linen; but the main part of the market is in an open square below the church where livestock is displayed for sale. Cages of rabbits, duckling, pullets, hens, turkeys and pigeons stand at the entrance whilst in the square itself are lambs, sheep, goats and kids, horses and mules. Farm machinery is also drawn up for sale. All the guide books advise you to go very early in the morning for this part of the market, but going at a more leisurely 9 to 10 am still reveals a lively group of countrymen in heated discussion over their sales and purchases.

At the large ANDRAITX market, one frequently sees an old man with cages of live hens, chickens, pigeons and rabbits. But as it is another popular tourist venue the large section devoted to gifts, clothes and leathergoods tends to dominate the food stalls.

For real country charm visit MANACOR, where there is a daily food market and the gifts, clothes and leathergoods are kept separate from this on Mondays. Freshly-killed wild rabbits, snails, bunches of dried herbs and home-made Majorcan sausages are displayed amongst the fruit and vegetables. The old man who sells you a kilo of rich-red sweet tomatoes he has grown himself hands them over with the words *Come bien* — eat well.

Majorcan Weekly Markets

Monday:	Caimari; Calviá; Llorita; Manacor; Montuiri
Tuesday:	Alcudia; Artá; Can Picafort; Llubi; Porreras; Santa Margarita; Can Pastilla
Wednesday:	Andraitx; Capdepera; Colonia de Sant Jordi; Port Pollensa; Sineu
Thursday:	Ariany; Campos; Consell; Can Pastilla; Inca; Sant Joan; Sant Llorenc; Ses Salines
Friday:	Alaró; Algaida; Llucmajor; Maria de la Salud; Son Servera
Saturday:	Bunyola; Cala Rajada; Campanet; Costitx; Lloseta; Son Ferriol; Santanyi; Soller
Sunday:	Alcudia; Binisalem; Felanitx; Muró; Pollensa; La Puebla; Santa Maria

BINISALEM
VINO DE LA TIERRA

José L. Ferrer

VINO DE MESA TINTO
ELABORADO, CRIADO Y EMBOTELLADO
POR: **FRANJA ROJA, S.A.** - BINISALEM - ESPAÑA

REG. EMB. 894 / P.M.   13 % Vol   70 cl.

CRIANZA 1985

A red wine bottle label from the bodega Jose L. Ferrer (see p 27)

WINES

In 1789, Geronimo de Berard, a Majorcan aristocrat, made a detailed study of the principal towns of Majorca in his *Viaje a las Villas de Mallorca*. He devoted particular attention to towns renowned for their vineyards. He remarked that the mountain village of Deya, on the north-west coast produced an *'exquisito vino'*; its neighbour, Valldemosa, a quantity of *Malvasia* (a sweet wine named for the variety of grape from which it is made); and Calviá (another village), a certain wine which he said was of better quality than that produced on the central plain. In his opinion, the very best Majorcan wines (*'los mas exquisitos vinos de la isla'*), were produced in the cliff-top coastal town of Banyalbufar.

None of these highly-praised wines were made in large quantities. It was in the towns of the central plain, Es Pla, that the bulk of Majorcan wine was produced. Reds predominated in the areas around Santa Maria, Consell, Binisalem and Sencellas. Binisalem was particularly noted for the high quality of its grapes, which produced a wine with excellent keeping qualities. Manacor, Porreras, and Felanitx were noted mainly for whites.

In 1868 the French vineyards were destroyed by phylloxera. All of Spain's wine regions benefited from the disaster, especially Majorca which developed a thriving wine export industry with France. In 1877, Majorcan wines won major prizes at an exhibition in Madrid, but this fame was short-lived. Phylloxera struck a few years later, reaching its climax in 1891, and by the time it had run its course a great many vineyards which could have been replanted with immune strains had been turned over to other crops.

Of the wine-producing areas described by Geronimo de Berard only those of the central plain have survived, with the red wines of Binisalem emerging as the best. The *'exquisito vino'* of the north-west coast is no longer produced commercially, although in the Estellenchs/Banyalbufar area an excellent *Malvasia* is still produced, privately and for private consumption only.

The growth of tourism, now the island's main industry, initially did little for the Majorcan wine trade as it caused the loss of some of the wine-producing land and diverted capital and labour into that more profitable channel. Also, the wines of mainland Spain were, and still are, dominant on hotel and restaurant menus and supermarket shelves. Fortunately, this state of affairs is changing. The quality of local wine is improving each year; and distribution and marketing methods are improving too.

The development of Majorcan wines is now supported by the Balearic government, which gives grants of 75% towards the plantation of new vines. The bank which runs the scheme has an expert to advise on the best varieties to plant.

All this sounds like small-scale activity, and it is. But in one respect, Majorca may claim the credit for one of the most important developments ever in world wine production. It was probably a Majorcan who established the first vineyards in California.

Fray Junipero Serra, the Franciscan friar who virtually founded California, was born in the Majorcan town of Petra in 1713 and left in 1749 with a group of Majorcan friars to convert the Indians in New Spain, which in those days included Mexico and Southern California. He founded some of the United States' most important west coast towns and cities including Los Angeles, San Francisco and San Diego. His success at converting the Indians was due largely to his knowledge of rural life and agricultural skills which enabled him to identify with Indian interests. It is thought that he took with him from Majorca the first vines to be planted in California. In the bodega of José Ferrer at Binisalem, there is a 200 year old grape press identical with one in a San Diego museum, which indicates some Majorcan influence in that area. Junipero Serra himself is considered to be the first pioneer in California and in the Washington Hall of Fame, he represents that State. He was beatified by Pope John Paul II in Rome on 25 September 1988.

If Majorca introduced viticulture to California, California has repaid the debt by exporting the North American technique of cool fermentation of white wine to Majorca. Indeed the cool fermentation room at José Ferrer's bodega made one wine writer think he was in California. Majorca is not noted for its white wines; the winters are not cold enough to produce anything other than flat, heavy whites. However, since the introduction of the new American technique, they are improving.

The very best Majorcan red wines are produced by José Ferrer of Binisalem. Bodegas José L. Ferrer (Franja Roja) (telephone 511050) can easily be found on the outskirts of Binisalem on the road from Palma. The office is open from 8 am to 12 pm and from 2 pm to 6 pm on weekdays for the sale of wine by the case and, as usual, wine bought from the source is cheaper than that bought in the shops. The principal grape used is the Manto Negro, although other varieties include Callet and Fogoneu. Prensall and Moll are the grapes used to produce white wines. Of the various reds, the Binisalem Autentico Joven Tinto is a very pleasant light wine, frequently served chilled in an earthenware jug in Majorcan restaurants. It is best drunk within a year.

The wine matured traditionally in oak casks at this bodega is labelled under the name José L. Ferrer together with the vintage date. Exceptionally good vintages are labelled '*Reserva*' or '*Gran Reserva*', plus the date. These are worth seeking out, for they are wines of great quality at very low prices. Other wines produced are a white (Binisalem Autentico José L. Ferrer) and a rosé (Binisalem Autentico José L. Ferrer).

Tours of this bodega are available during the stated office hours, but it is necessary to telephone to make arrangements and you need to speak Spanish. The same applies to most other bodegas.

The Bodega de Felanitx is a sprawling, untidy complex on the outskirts of the simple, timeless agricultural town of Felanitx, whose medieval origins are still apparent in the narrow winding streets around the central covered market. The bodega is a co-operative of most of the farmers of the region. Louis Ripoll in his *Libre de Vins, Licors i per necessari* puts the number of members at about 520. Felanitx mainly produces a light everyday wine, the sort Majorcans mix with water or *gaseosa* at lunchtime, and has been overshadowed by Binisalem. Foganeu is the principal grape used for whites; Callet, Manto Negro and Garnacha for reds.

The co-operative is also one of the major producers of dried apricots on the island. The area is famous for its apricot orchards and the bodega is a pleasure to visit in the first week of July, just for the sight of rich orange apricots stretched across a huge yard, drying in the sun.

The Bodega de Felanitx is found in calle Guillermo Timoner (telephone 580110). Its red, white and rosé wines are marketed under the names C. Santeuri, Felanitx, La Viña, La Cepas, and 1919 (the year in which the co-operative was founded). A red wine of *Reserva* quality is also made.

Vinos Oliver, calle Font 26, Petra, (telephone 291612) make a rosé, Celler son Calo, from locally grown Foganeu and Manto Negro grapes. They also make from Manto Negro and Gueferró grapes a red, Mont Ferrutx, which is matured in oak casks. These giant casks are just discernible in the gloom as you peer through the barred openings in the old, thick-walled bodega, and the sleepy street is pervaded by the rich smell of wine fermenting in oak.

In addition, there are two very small concerns making wine from Majorcan grapes. Vins Prensall, calle Son Boy 21, Consell (telephone 622119) make white, rosé and red wines under the name Vins Prensall. Prensall grapes are used for the white and Manto Negro and Callet for the rosé and red. Vins d'Or, calle Gremio Albañiles 22, Palma, make red wines labelled Vins d'Or Reserva and Gran Reserva, also using Manto Negro and Callet grapes.

It is worthwhile making a note of these Majorcan wines as they are very pleasant and inexpensive. Restaurants specialising in Majorcan dishes usually carry a range of them, but rarely distinguish them from mainland wines on their lists.

The Majorcan wines of José Ferrer have become available for the first time in the UK: all enquiries should be made to the sole importer, The Four Vintners, 7 Kingsland Road, London E2 8AA (telephone 01 739 7335).

LIQUEURS

The distillation of liqueurs (*aquardientes*) in Majorca is deeply rooted in tradition. Originally they were produced from private stills or by cottage industries using basic methods which give the liqueur from each still its own personal characteristics. Unfortunately, the liqueurs produced in Majorca today are totally different; since they are produced commercially and controlled by industrial law, they have a uniform flavour. Of the many produced privately in the past, only two are now made commercially.

PALO is very popular, usually drunk as an aperetif, with a little soda water and ice. It is black in colour. The commercial exploitation of Palo, a liqueur indigenous to Majorca, started in Lluchmayor over 80 years ago. It is made with quinine boiled with sorrel roots, pure grape alcohol and burnt sugar.

HIERBAS (sweet or dry: *dulce o seca*) is Majorcan though it is also manufactured in Ibiza. Hierbas used to be made only by a few private houses and farms from recipes handed down through the families, using the herbs and vegetation to hand. It is, even now, only made in the month of May. Its ingredients are alcohol flavoured with aniseed, to which the following herbs are added: peppermint (bark, flowers and leaves), fennel, camomile, rosemary, winter savory, mint, lavender, oregano, and rue. When this distillation is bottled, orange and lemon flowers, lemon leaves, linden, eucalyptus, bay and olive leaves and some carob are added to each bottle; these help to give the liqueur its soft green colour and add to the flavour and aroma. Hierbas is drunk at any time of the day in bars and after meals.

MISTELA, a sweet liqueur, is made at the Bodega de Felanitx, using very old distillation methods but only when circumstances are favourable. Alas, it is never sold to the public, being reserved solely for members of the co-operative. This is the remnant of what was once a major industry in Felanitx. In 1789 Geronimo de Berard listed Felanitx as having 60 stills, the largest number on the island, in order to make their famous rich liqueur (*'el rico aquardiente tan celebrado'*).

29

TAPAS

Tapas are tiny plates of food served in bars all over Spain to accompany drinks. The word *tapa* means lid. Although no-one is really sure of the origin of this institution, it is thought that bars started to offer morsels of food with their drinks to attract custom (a procedure which was echoed later on in Australia). Anna MacMiadhacháin, in her book *Spanish Regional Cookery,* gives another plausible explanation of their origin; she speculates that they are a legacy of the Moorish occupation of Spain, when the serving of alcohol was forbidden except with food.

Nowadays the custom of giving free *tapas* is dying out, but the idea of selling them has really caught on. True *tapas* are still served on miniature plates which hold just a few bites of food, half a dozen mussels, for example, or a few meatballs, and the Spanish custom is to have one plate of something with a beer or a glass of wine. Some bars now specialise in *tapas* and here they serve larger portions so that with a variety of dishes you can make up a meal. This is a popular idea with tourists, who can see the food on display in the bar before ordering and know more or less what they are getting.

Each region produces *tapas* which reflect its own cooking style. Since these can sometimes be quite complicated to prepare and cook, and since an essential feature of *tapas* is variety, they are only to be found in bars and restaurants.

In Majorca, as in all the other regions, dishes that are popular in *tapas* bars may appear as a first or second course in the home; or may be served as appetisers with drinks before a meal. However, *tapas* as a meal or form of entertaining never feature in domestic cooking. The present vogue for giving *tapas* parties, which has been fostered by books on the subject in the USA, would come as a real surprise to Majorcans!

THE PIG AND ITS PRODUCTS

The basis of much Majorcan cookery is the pig, *el porc* in Mallorquin, *el cerdo* in Castilian. The prominence of this animal gave fuel to George Sand's defamatory writing about the island.

'The pig allows no waste, he lets nothing be lost; and is the finest example of prodigal voracity, combined with simplicity of tastes and habits, that can be offered to the nations of the world. Hence he came to enjoy in Majorca rights and privileges which nobody had so far dreamed of offering to humans. Houses have been enlarged and ventilated; the fruit which used to rot on the ground has been gathered, sorted and stored; and steamships, previously considered needless and unreasonable, now run between Majorca and the mainland.

'It was therefore entirely thanks to the hog that I could visit the island; had I entertained the idea of going there three years before, the prospects of so long and hazardous a journey by coaster would have made me abandon it. But, with the export of hogs, civilisation has made its impression on Majorca.'

Los Embutidos (pork sausages)

Until fairly recent times, nearly every family raised a pig to be killed during the cool winter months from November to February to provide basic meat supplies and lard for cooking. Because the preserving of meat in a warm and humid climate is difficult without refrigeration, much of the meat from a slaughtered pig was made into various sausages. Some of these sausages, because of the spices used, would keep for a year, and became fundamental to many Majorcan dishes. The wide use, especially of *sobrasada* (an unusual and acquired taste) is one reason why Majorcan dishes are difficult to reproduce outside Majorca and the Spanish mainland where they are also available.

Among the poorer families, the fresh meat made available on the days of the *matanza de cerdo,* as the pig killing *fiesta* is called, was the only fresh meat they ate, apart from small birds netted or trapped during the winter. Their diet consisted almost entirely of home-grown vegetables, bread and pork sausages. The great importance of the sausages is demonstrated by the fact that they used to feature as valuable properties in wills and dowry contracts. Commenting on one particular will, of 1568, in which some bacon and a number of pork sausages were left by a father to his daughter, a recent historian remarked that this bequest implied terrible poverty and hunger at the time. Not so, in my opinion; it just showed the importance of these products of the pig.

The *matanzas* in Majorca are not now what they used to be; the practice is in decline, though there are still some families who keep a pig and follow the old traditions. The old two day *fiesta* is now more likely to be a one day affair, and the pig killed will rarely be an authentic black pig, *el cerdo negro mallorquin.*

This Majorcan black pig is a variety of Iberian pig which is distinguished from other breeds by its high fat content. This, and its traditional diet of dried and fresh figs, prickly pear, barley and boiled sweet potatoes are the reason for the fame of Majorcan sausages. But nowadays, the pigs generally bred are of the kind known as Large White, which has a fashionably lower fat content, or a cross between the black and the white; and sausages from these pigs are inferior. Another reason for the decline in quality of the sausages is that most of them are now factory-made, often with inferior meat and chemical additives.

Fortunately, a campaign for real Majorcan sausages is being waged, led by Sebastian Simo Planes, the owner of Ca'n Tia, which so far as I know is the only shop selling authentic Majorcan sausages. These are made in the traditional way, using natural spices and prime cuts of pork from black pigs fed on natural foods; and the pigs are free-range, not confined to sties. Ca'n Tia is in Palma, close to the town hall on the edge of the Plaza Cort. I recommend buying Majorcan sausages there and nowhere else. The difference is as noticeable as that between home-baked and mass-produced bread.

In the following account of various kinds of sausage and other pork products, the Majorcan name precedes the Castilian one in the sub-headings, but I have used the more familiar Castilian name in the text.

SOBRASSADA, *sobrasada*

The most famous of the Majorcan sausages, *sobrasada* is irregularly shaped, soft, spicy and reddish-orange. It can be eaten raw and is a popular snack spread on bread. Authentic *sobrasada* contains cuts of meat from the loin, fillet and leg, all finely chopped and mixed with about 25 g (1 oz) of salt and 40 g (2 oz) of mild paprika, *pimenton mallorquin* (p 46), to the kilo. Cayenne pepper is added but the amount varies, depending on how spicy the sausage is to be; it is sold in a mild and spicy version. Its size also varies depending on the size of the intestine into which the pork mixture is stuffed. Hung in a cool, draught-free place, *sobrasada* will keep for a year. To show this, at the *fiesta* to celebrate the killing of the current pig it was (and still is) traditional to serve some of the *sobrasada* from the previous year.

Sobrasada must never be kept in the refrigerator but hung in a cool place.

LLANGONISSA, *longaniza*

This variety of *sobrasada* is a long, thin, orange-red sausage in the form of a single coil with the two ends tied together. Majorcans love to have country picnics in the winter, at which they enjoy these sausages barbecued over a wood fire. Or they may cut them into ordinary sausage lengths and fry them with eggs. A *longaniza* does not have the keeping qualities of the regular *sobrasada;* it should not be stored in the refrigerator but hung in a cool place and used within two or three months of purchase.

BUTIFARRÓ, *butifarron*

In shape and size, the *butifarron* is very similar to an ordinary English sausage though the colour of its natural casing can vary from grey to black. It is a delicious blood sausage spiced with cinnamon, fennel seeds and black pepper and is so popular that it is commercially manufactured throughout the year. It used to be only a winter sausage, produced from November to February.

Butifarron should not be refrigerated as this can alter the flavour. Store instead in a cool place but, in any case, eat within three days of purchase. As these sausages are pre-cooked, they can be eaten as they are with bread, but they also make an excellent addition to vegetable and pulse dishes as well as to some meat stews.

BUTIFARRA, *butifarra*

The large version of *butifarron,* this resembles a small haggis in appearance. Serve it sliced, as it is, with bread or boil it whole with meat or vegetables then cut it into slices and serve everything together, hot.

CAMAIOT, *camaiot*

Though a similar mixture to the *butifarra,* it contains less blood and has a firmer, coarser texture. The meat is diced rather than finely chopped and there is a higher fat content. The *camaiot* has a curious, irregular shape; it is sewn with string into a piece of the pig's skin and weighs about 1 kilo (2 ¼ lb). It can be served sliced with other cold meats, diced and added to meat stews or vegetable dishes or even boiled whole with other ingredients and served hot, cut into slices. It has excellent keeping qualities for up to one year if hung in a cool place. Never refrigerate.

Other Pork Products

PERNIL, jamón serrano, serrano ham
Majorca's warm climate and high humidity mean that they cannot produce ham. This is a mountain ham from the Spanish mainland which is much used in Majorcan cookery these days. Grocer's shops, butchers', supermarkets, all sell serrano ham, which should be very thinly sliced — it is often served with cheese and olives as *tapas* with drinks. Offcuts and the bones are sold cheaply to flavour soups, stews, and vegetable or pulse casserole dishes.

XULLA, tocino, pork fat
This is salted pork fat that can be finely chopped and added to stuffings, diced into stews or boiled whole with meat and sausages or vegetables, sliced and served hot. It is very popular and can be purchased at butchers' shops, cold meat counters and frequently at market stalls that sell other preserved products such as salt cod, olives and pickled vegetables. *Tocino fresco* or fresh pork fat, bought from butchers' shops, is also widely used.

SAIM DE PORC, manteca de cerdo, lard
Lard was formerly used a great deal in Majorcan cookery but nowadays olive oil is increasingly being substituted. In the recipes I often give a choice by listing lard or olive oil in the list of ingredients; where lard appears on its own, this means that it is necessary to the dish.

Majorca is not known for its dairy produce, and butter only became generally available in the 1970's with the advent of mass tourism. I know a number of Majorcan families who wouldn't know what to do with butter if you gave it to them and any Majorcan recipes using butter are either very modern or pinched from the neighbouring island of Minorca. That island is well known for its dairy produce, especially cheese, and butter is a common ingredient in the local dishes there.

PLANT FOODS

Olives, aceitunas, olives

Huge baskets of fresh, green olives start to appear in all the shops late in September. Many people still use their old family recipes to cure them, with a large quantity of fennel. The result is an acquired taste, since the olives retain some of their bitterness and the fennel is strong. Recipes vary from household to household and the one which follows is derived from various sources.

Clean the dust and bits of leaves from the olives and hit each one with a wooden mallet to split the flesh in order to allow the brine to penetrate — make sure you are wearing old clothes or an apron as this can be messy.

Soak the split olives in a bowl of water for an hour. Meanwhile prepare your brine by using a wooden spoon to stir coarse salt into water (about 110 g/3 oz, to 1 litre/36 fl oz of water) until it dissolves. Make sure that you have enough of this brine to cover the olives. Now remove the olives from their bowl, drain them, and put them in a glass or porcelain container, with brine to cover and with plenty of fresh sprigs of fennel and some thyme, as well as lemon leaves, bay leaves and whole garlic cloves; as much or as little as you like. Top each container with a layer of fennel, thyme and lemon leaves; and then wedge a cross of thick twigs over the leaves to ensure that the uppermost olives are held down and remain immersed in brine. Do not cover the container as the olives should be allowed to breathe.

Curing time varies a lot according to the size and the ripeness of the olives. They can be sampled after 21 days but they may take up to 6 months to really soak up flavour. Always use a wooden spoon to remove olives from the container, never your hands as these would introduce bacteria to the brine. If any grey patches appear on the brine, just skim them off; they are perfectly harmless, just oil from the olives.

Black olives, which are ripened green olives, start to appear in the shops in late November and are much easier to deal with. If very ripe, they only need to be sprinkled with salt and good olive oil and left to marinate with a few peeled garlic cloves for a few hours before eating; but all black olives benefit from a few days to a few weeks in the marinade. Again, always use a wooden spoon when removing olives from their glass or porcelain container.

Oli d'oliva, aceite de oliva, olive oil
The gnarled, ancient olive trees are a striking feature in many areas of the island. Caimari, a small town about six kilometres to the north of Inca, is the home of the largest olive oil plant on the island, but there are many small local presses all over the island who will accept a single sack of olives for pressing. If you have less than this, they will press your olives with those of other non-farmers and divide the oil according to weight.

Two kinds of oil are usually available for sale. *Aceite de oliva virgen extra,* oil from the first pressing of the olives, is slightly green in colour and has a strong flavour. It is best used in a dressing for salads, cooked vegetables and meats, in mayonnaise or in any dish where the flavour of olive oil is important. The other, *aceite de oliva pura* is lighter with a clearer golden colour. It is a blend of *virgen* and refined olive oil and is used in deep frying and in general cooking where the distinctive flavour of olive oil is not desired.

The origin of mayonnaise, the sauce most generally associated with olive oil, is obscure. In Spain, they believe that mayonnaise originated in the Balearic island of Minorca, but there are a number of other countries which claim to have created it. Majorcans, and Catalan people generally (and, indeed, Italians and Greeks too), use a special container for pouring oil in the specific way required for making mayonnaise. Known as an *aceitera* and looking, in the old-fashioned tin version, rather like a mechanic's oil can, it is nowadays found in a disposable plastic version. Litre containers of olive oil and sunflower oil are sold in plastic *aceiteras,* complete with handle and fine spout.

Though a blender will make mayonnaise quickly in a domestic kitchen, preparing small quantities by hand is satisfying and, once you have the hang of it, a quick process. I give a recipe on page 48.

Bledes, acelgas, Swiss chard
This is a mild-tasting green leaf vegetable, similar to spinach, for

which it can be substituted, though it has a firmer texture. It is used in a wide variety of Majorcan dishes.

Albercoc, albaricoques, apricots

To end a meal with a bowl of ripe, freshly-picked apricots, warmly scented and succulently sweet, is one of the joys of a Majorcan summer. Yet in this natural state, they are little appreciated by the local population, for they fetch just a few pesetas a kilo.

But considerable value is added to the fruits by drying them naturally in the sun. These sun-dried apricots command high prices and are greatly sought after as a delicacy by people in other countries. In Majorca itself, a popular winter dessert in both homes and restaurants is a simple plate of locally dried apricots and some recently harvested almonds.

One of the largest apricot growing areas is the gently undulating, fertile land surrounding the inland towns of Felanitx and Porreras. A constantly changing patchwork of colour, in late June and throughout July, at the time of the apricot harvest, it is vivid with burnt orange, gold and terracotta contrasted by the strong greens of the vineyards, evergreen oaks, olive trees and the apricot orchards. Tourists are few and are mainly seen at the big Sunday market held every week in and around the enormous market hall of Felanitx.

It takes approximately 5 kilos of fresh apricots to make one kilo of dried ones. On a hot July weekday, the steady stream of small tractors pulling carts laden with freshly gathered apricots into the various towns and villages is the area's chief activity. Most are destined for the many apricot-drying installations that abound; one can hardly call them factories or plants as most are no bigger than a garage. Here, apricots are halved and stoned by hand and laid out to dry in the sun.

Only the Bodega de Felanitx is partially mechanised. It is better known for its wine production; dried apricots are just one of a number of profitable sidelines for this farmers' co-operative. The production from this bodega is the biggest I have seen, and the installation of a machine which successfully halves and stones the fruit has removed one very tedious job. However, the rest of the work is still done by hand. The noisy Heath Robinson machine spits out the stoned halves onto a conveyor belt where they are lined up by the wives and teenage children of the co-operative members. They place the apricots, cut side up, into shallow wooden trays.

After being stacked overnight, the trays of apricots are spread out in the sun, brilliant orange against the beige wood and neutral stone of the large yard, for just half a day before being restacked in tall columns to protect them from any further drying by the sun. For the next three days, these columns are placed in the open yard to complete the drying process in the warm air.

Exporting starts at the end of August. Shipments go as far away as New Zealand and continue until December, but there are still plenty of naturally dried apricots available for local consumption. These are a product of the co-operatives, who do not go in for expensive brand name packaging. So when buying in Majorca, look for dried apricots packed simply in polystyrene trays covered with cling film and with an accompanying label stating that they are packed in Majorca. So tender are they that they need no cooking and can be eaten just as they are.

Ametillas, almendras, almonds
There are several million almond trees all over the island and in February the almond groves in blossom are very beautiful. In August, small gangs of workers, often gypsies, move around the island to help with the harvest. Vast green nets are spread out under the trees, which are then beaten with sticks to make them give up their crop of nuts. The sharp clacking sound made by striking the trees is as distinctive as the cicadas on a hot summer day.

The outer husks are removed and used as fuel during the winter. The husked nuts are sent off to the local nut-cracking factory, usually a small concern, where the shells are removed by machine. As cultivation and harvesting are so labour intensive, almonds are almost as expensive in Majorca as in Britain but those bought in Majorca are much fresher — even those offered for sale in late July or early August, when they are almost a year old. About 80% of the harvest is exported.

Plant Foods

Majorca accounts for about two thirds of the total almond production in Spain.

Almonds are much used in Majorcan cooking for thickening stews and sauces as well as in a wide range of sweet dishes for Christmas and special *fiestas*.

Setas, wild mushrooms

Several kinds of edible fungi grow wild on the island. From late October to January, it is a popular pastime to go looking for them. However, you have to know what to look for; if you are unsure it is best to buy them. The most popular of the edible wild fungi are *esclats-sang,* a kind of 'milk-cap'. They are orange-brown in colour with touches of green, and I am told that their scientific name is *Lactarius sanguifluus.*

In season, wild mushrooms, some of which are called *bolets* locally, are widely available, but extremely expensive. I learned the reason why one December when I was taken on a mush-room-gathering expedition. As most of Majorca's land is in private hands we had to pay an entrance fee — it is quite normal to see signs forbidding the gathering of *setas* and areas where they can be found for free are crowded at weekends. We went to the lower slopes of the Galatzo Mountain, for *setas* enjoy growing in hilly and mountainous regions. Though fun in the warm December sunshine, it was a thorny and unrewarding outing; the number of *setas* found did not cover the entrance fee.

Setas are considered essential in a number of dishes, especially *arroz brut* and *sopas de matances* (see pp 68 and 62 respectively). Lightly fried in a little olive oil with a *picada* of chopped parsley and garlic, they are served with mixed grilled meats and sausages and are a regular accompaniment with pork.

Tomàtigas, tomates, tomatoes

It is hard to imagine any Spanish cooking without the tomato; at least one always seems to be required somewhere in the course of a cooking operation.

The basis for many Spanish dishes is the *sofrito,* a preparation made from onions or spring onions, olive oil and tomatoes in which other ingredients are then cooked. It is one of the few basic preparations common to the whole of Spain. The Majorcans use

42

43

it in nearly every savoury dish. It is interesting that those magnificent large Mediterranean spring onions, which they often use with or instead of onions in a *sofrito,* are known in Mallorquin as *sofrit.*

Mediterranean grown tomatoes are large and juicy, each one weighing about 200 g (7 oz) or more. When they are not at their best, in the winter and spring, people turn to the vast range of tinned tomatoes and tomato sauces, or to *tomates de ramilletes,* tiny tomatoes stored strung together on a string. Two or three of these can be substituted for one large summer tomato.

The tinned tomato products are excellent, but some of the sauces, especially the various makes of the highly popular *tomate frito,* have a cloying, commercial taste and are best avoided. This sauce was, and still is, made at home in the summer months, when tomatoes are plentiful, and would keep a year in a cool, dark larder.

See the tomato sauce recipes on page 49.

HERBS AND SPICES

There are a number of specialist shops for herbs and spices (Mallorquin, *herbes i especies:* Castilian *hierbas y especias*) in Palma where all herbs and spices mentioned in the recipes can be bought loose by the gram — the best way to buy them. The three best known shops are close together at the far end (from Plaza Mayor) of calle Sindicato. Another excellent shop is in calle Dameto Servet opposite the Santa Catalina market. Small bunches of mixed fresh herbs in season are offered for sale in most markets and at some of the larger supermarkets.

All, ajo, garlic
Garlic, an essential seasoning in Majorcan cooking, is used in numerous ways; the whole unpeeled head can be added to a dish; or whole cloves, either peeled or unpeeled; or the cloves can first be crushed or finely chopped. In late spring and early summer the garlic plant (*ajo tierno*), looking rather like a spring onion, is available and worth trying for its light garlic flavour, either finely chopped in salads or in cooked dishes. The garlic bulbs should be firm and crisp — the fresher the garlic, the milder the taste. Yellowing, soft cloves and any which are starting to sprout should be discarded.

Taperes, alcaparras, capers
Capers are the small, unripe fruit of a bushy plant that grows extensively in the Mediterranean. Of Majorca's crop, 75% is exported. On the island itself, they are widely used as an addition to meat and vegetable dishes, salads and sauces. An unusual caper, the *alcaparron,* which closely resembles a gooseberry, is worth seeking out. Pickled in wine vinegar, its sharp taste goes well with cold meats, in salads and with drinks — served as one would olives.

Pickled vegetables are regularly served with drinks or first courses in Majorcan households, and specialist stalls at markets and supermarkets sell a range of these.

Islacapers of Felanitx is the best known Majorcan firm, exporting widely not just capers but various pickled vegetables, and their products are easily available in Majorca.

45

Fonoll, hinojo, fennel
Fennel grows wild and in abundance all over the island. Its distinctive flavour can be discerned in many dishes, though not in fish dishes, which is odd, for the flavour of fennel combined with fish is common elsewhere in the Mediterranean. There is no need ever to buy supplies of fennel — just pick it from the side of the road, of course.

Llorer, laurel, bay
Sold fresh in untidy bunches at supermarkets and vegetable stalls. A common ingredient in vegetable dishes. Be warned: Spanish *laurel* is not the same as English laurel, which is poisonous.

Julivert, perejil, parsley
The parsley grown in Majorca is not the curly-leafed kind familiar in Britain. It has a flat, more definite leaf and a more pungent flavour. It is the most common herb used in Majorcan cooking, and is sold by the (large) bunch at market vegetable stalls and supermarkets everywhere.

Picat, picada
A mixture, usually of chopped parsley and garlic, which is added to many fish and meat dishes towards the end of cooking time.

In Catalan cuisine, almonds are included in *picada,* and other variations exist. Patience Gray in *Honey from a Weed* explains its purpose:

> The real function of *picada* in its diverse forms is the final unification of the various ingredients and the liaison of the sauce without recourse to flour; it produces a more subtle result.

Pebrebord, pimenton rojo, mild paprika
An essential spice in Majorcan cookery, used in large quantities. It is ground from the dried, sweet red capsicum and is not hot but imparts a mild, distinctive flavour to the food. The very best paprika is *pimenton mallorquin,* locally produced using natural methods.

Pimenton mallorquin was originally made from home-grown sweet peppers, dried naturally in the sun and ground by hand.

Few families now bother to make their own, but a number of small firms in Majorca have started to produce it by the old method. This product is very expensive, but essential to the production of the renowned Majorcan sausage called *sobrasada*, for it contains no chemicals or additives of any kind that could taint and even lessen the life of the sausage, and the flavour is far superior to any commercial paprika. It is one of the reasons why authentic *sobrasadas* such as those produced by Ca'n Tia are more expensive than the factory versions. The various spice shops in Palma's calle Sindicato sell *pimenton mallorquin*, especially during the winter months, in great quantities.

Safró, azafran, saffron
This precious spice is so intimately connected with rice that I have dealt with it in the Rice chapter (p 65).

Tot especies, todas especias, spice mixture
A homemade mixture of equal quantities of ground cinnamon, black peppercorns and cloves, a generous pinch of which is frequently added to casserole dishes of meat or vegetables at the end of cooking time.

SALSA MAHONESA

Salsa mayonesa   Mayonnaise

Older cooks still make mayonnaise with a large pestle and mortar but a bowl and wooden spoon will do just as well. For successful mayonnaise, all the ingredients, the eggs, the oil and the mixing bowl must be at room temperature.

3 egg yolks   275 ml (10 fl oz)
lemon juice   virgin olive oil
salt

Beat the egg yolks with a few drops of lemon juice and a pinch of salt and then beat in the oil drop by drop until the sauce begins to emulsify. At this point, you can start to add the oil in a thin stream, beating all the time. When all the oil is incorporated, flavour with more lemon juice and salt if necessary. If your mixture curdles, put an egg yolk into another basin, add some oil drop by drop until it starts to emulsify and then beat in the curdled mixture very slowly, then the remainder of the oil.

ALLIOLI

Ajoaceite   Aiolli

2 egg yolks   275 ml (10 fl oz)
5 peeled garlic cloves   virgin olive oil
salt   lemon juice

Crush the garlic cloves with a little salt and then add the egg yolks, making sure that they are all mixed together. Using a wooden spoon, beat in the oil drop by drop until the sauce begins to emulsify, then add the oil in a steady thin stream. When all the oil is incorporated, flavour with some lemon juice and a little more salt if necessary.

TOMATIGA FRITA

Tomate frito   Tomato sauce (to keep)

5 kg (11-12 lb) large, ripe   a few large sprigs of
  tomatoes   parsley
1 head garlic   salt
¼ litre (9 fl oz) olive oil   black pepper

Wash the tomatoes and cut them up roughly. Peel and lightly crush the garlic cloves. Heat the olive oil in a casserole, preferably of earthenware, and fry the garlic cloves until light golden in colour; then add the tomatoes, salt, pepper and parsley. Simmer until the tomatoes have reduced by half. Then sieve the mixture, pour it into clean glass jars, cover with a thin layer of virgin olive oil and seal.

Place the jars in a large saucepan filled with cold water. Bring slowly to the boil and simmer for 20 minutes. (A tip one old cook gave me was to tuck a tea towel over the tops of the jars to prevent them from banging together as they boiled). Cool in the water and then store in a cool, dark spot. Just reheat to serve as a simple sauce, or add to any dish that requires a tomato sauce.

SALSA DE TOMATIGA

Salsa de tomate   Tomato sauce

1 kg (2¼ lb) ripe tomatoes   some roughly chopped
1 small onion   fresh parsley
4 cloves garlic   salt
125 ml (4½ fl oz) olive oil   ground white pepper

Wash and roughly chop the tomatoes; peel and chop the onion and garlic cloves. Heat the oil in a large saucepan and add the onion and garlic. Just before they begin to take colour, add the tomatoes, parsley and seasoning. Cook on a fairly high heat, stirring frequently, until the tomatoes have thickened and formed a purée. Pass the sauce through a sieve or vegetable mill and reheat before serving.

49

SPECIAL UTENSILS

Earthenware cooking pots
The traditional earthenware used in cooking is still very popular and reasonably cheap. Though not necessary (I myself can detect little difference between food cooked in earthenware and that cooked in metal), these pots are a pleasure to use; they can be brought directly to the table, where they retain heat exceptionally well; and they give an authentic look to Majorcan food.

They do, however, require special treatment when first purchased. All earthenware pots should be soaked for 24 hours in cold water — this will prevent them from soaking up any of the cooking liquid when first used — and then filled with cold water and brought very slowly to the boil. After this the water is thrown away, effectively removing any dusty, clay-like taste from the pots, and they are ready for use.

A *greixonera* is a shallower earthenware vessel with four small handles and a rounded bottom, bearing some resemblance to a Chinese wok, and is available in various sizes including an enormous catering size for use in restaurants. The name *greixonera,* which is Mallorquin for casserole, is given to a number of dishes which are traditionally cooked in one, and it is widely used as a name for sauces and stews. Of all the kinds of earthenware pot, this is probably the most useful to have.

Because of the way 'casserole dishes' have evolved in Britain and elsewhere, many people think of a 'casserole' as something which has a lid. So I should explain that the *greixonera* does not come with a lid. If a lid is called for in a recipe, Majorcans would either use a slightly smaller and shallower greixonera, which would fit on top, or large cabbage leaves.

A typical *greixonera* is shown bottom left in the drawing on the page opposite.

Special Utensils

Pestle and mortar

A good pestle and mortar are invaluable. It is true that an electric grinder will do most of the working of grinding spices, nuts and seeds. However, when crushing garlic with fresh herbs or making a paste of nuts, spices, herbs and bread to add to a sauce as a thickening agent, the mortar is indispensable, achieving just the right texture.

Most Majorcan mortars are ceramic with a wooden pestle and it is best to buy a fairly large one, for some of the pastes to be pounded are quite substantial. The Majorcans make some of their sauces in mortars, especially mayonnaise and aiolli (p 48), so large ones are quite common.

Vegetable mill

This is an important utensil for purées and sauces. An electric blender can be used instead but may produce too smooth a texture for certain dishes. The vegetable mill gives a coarser finish, better suited to the simple and rustic style of cooking.

La plancha

This is an iron plate on which various foods are cooked. It is a favourite Spanish technique to cook meat, fish, eggs and vegetables directly on this hot, oiled plate. It derives from the not so distant past when all cooking was done on wood-burning stoves with a built-in hot plate.

Now that most people use the more convenient bottled butane gas or electricity, wood-burning stoves are a rarity. Separate *planchas* to fit on top of a gas burner or electric plate can be bought in kitchen shops; or a large, heavy-bottomed frying pan can be used instead.

A *plancha* requires some practice to use properly and, even in restaurants I have sometimes had food, especially vegetables, ruined by careless cooking on the *plancha* which has left the food either burnt or unevenly cooked.

Knives

Good sharp knives for various purposes are, obviously, important in any kind of cookery.

In Majorca, one special sort of knife worth looking out for in

an ironmonger's shop (*ferreteria*), and especially on ironmongers'
stalls at open air markets, is a small curved one rather like a
miniature scimitar. It is the traditional knife for cutting the
round, hard-crusted local bread — the bread is held to the body
whilst a slice is cut off by pulling the knife towards you. Most
Majorcans slice bread this way, even without the special knife.
Though it seems dangerous, it is in fact much safer than
attempting to slice the hard bread with a sharp knife on a bread
board.

These are the earthenware pots used to make aufegat. *For a full explanation of
their use see p 182.*

RECIPES

Introduction to the Recipes

I give the recipes in authentic Majorcan versions, since I think that people will prefer these to adaptations. However, although most Majorcan ingredients are fairly easy to find in, say, London or in North American cities where there is a Hispanic influence (not least New York City!), some readers may be unable to obtain everything they want. So I have sometimes suggested substitutes, where I am satisfied that their use does not rob a dish of its Majorcan flavour; but otherwise I think it better to let readers decide, if they have to, what changes to make.

Two matters need further explanation.

First, the utensils. If I recommend the use of a *greixonera* (p 51), because that is what Majorcans use, this is not to say that a similar dish from somewhere else will not serve the purpose. It is a good idea to use earthenware if possible, and to have the shape and size about right. But the *greixonera* is just a local form of a vessel which is found in many places in closely similar shapes and sizes. If, for example, you have bought earthenware cooking vessels which come from Portugal or the south of Italy or North Africa, they will probably be similar to the Majorcan ones.

Secondly, fish, indeed seafood in general. A first glance round a Majorcan fish market may suggest that the seafoods on display are peculiar to the Mediterranean. However, the fact is that most of the species found in the Mediterranean do occur elsewhere, for example in the North Atlantic, at least as far north as the Bay of Biscay and often further. One example is the red mullet, which is often thought of as being specially Mediterranean, but which comes up as far as the south coast of England. Anyway, fish offer plenty of scope for legitimate substitutions, so long as one has some understanding of the families in which they are grouped.

There are some exceptions. The Mediterranean scorpion fish (*cap roig* in Majorca, more familiar to many people under its

French name *rascasse*) is one; and the cleaver wrasse (*roar* in Majorca) another. But these are few.

I have one other general comment. Anyone setting out, as I have done, to record what is 'authentic' is going to have a natural bias in favour of the past — recipes set down in previous centuries, those imparted by elderly people, etc. And it would be absurd to present recently imported fashions such as American hamburgers, or 'with chips' dishes made for the benefit of British tourists, as if they were part of the 'real' Majorcan cuisine.

But Majorcan cuisine evolves. There was a time when it did not possess the tomato, for example. It would be an error to think solely in terms of the past and to ignore what is happening now; for that will be 'history' tomorrow. So in writing about the long-standing traditions of Majorca I have made some comments on the current situation.

WEIGHTS AND MEASURES
On weights and measures, I have used the metric system but given equivalences. I have avoided pints and cups, since the American ones are not the same as British ones, and used fluid ounces instead; it is not difficult to find a measuring cup which has these marked on it.

RECIPE TITLES
Each recipe has three titles: the Majorcan in the centre, Castilian Spanish (used in most Majorcan restaurants) below to the left, and English below to the right. There are indexes in all three languages, so it should always be possible to locate any of the dishes.

HOW MANY SERVINGS?
All recipes are meant for 4 people unless otherwise stated. If they are only suitable as a first course or a light main course, this is said.

Sopes: Bread-cum-Vegetable Dishes

The Majorcan word *sopes* has misled many foreigners into thinking that they were ordering a soup. Actually, *sopes* are thin slices of Majorcan country bread, *pan payes,* a circular, beige-coloured bread made from wheat; this bread is left unsalted, a tradition said to date from the Moorish occupation. Bakeries (*panaderias*) and grocers' shops (*colmados*) usually sell bags of pre-sliced *sopas,* but if you have some bread that is two or three days old, simply shave off thin slices and leave them in a cardboard box for 24-48 hours. This is much better than packet *sopas.*

There is no one 'correct' recipe for this simple and sustaining peasant dish, which consists basically of bread and cabbage but has many variations. However, here is a representative version.

SOPES MALLORQUINAS

Sopas mallorquinas   Majorcan bread and
con verduras   cabbage dish

In a *greixonera* (p 51), heat sufficient olive oil to fry some sliced leeks, garlic and spring onions. Add some skinned and chopped tomatoes and, when a thickish sauce has formed, a small green cabbage cut into very thin strips. Pour in some water and simmer until the cabbage is soft. Season with salt and pepper and incorporate the *sopas* in such a way that the cabbage remains on top. Make sure you add enough bread to soak up all the liquid. Add a good dash of olive oil, remove from the heat and allow to stand for a while until all the broth is absorbed.

The result is then sliced like cake, for it is nearly all bread.

I must add that this is not at all in keeping with present day tastes. Nowadays, restaurants use less bread so that the dish is more liquid. It is only in Majorcan homes that you would occasionally find a *sopas mallorquinas* that is mainly bread.

If you prefer to add less bread than the amounts I suggest in some of the following recipes, the best plan is to follow the restaurant technique: place the slices of bread, as much or as little as you like, in soup bowls and pour the vegetables on top.

PAMBOLI

Pa amb oli   Bread with oil

This is, literally, bread with oil. A slice of *pan payes* is sprinkled with salt and olive oil is then drizzled on top. It is served as a traditional breakfast or morning snack. Sometimes a cut tomato is rubbed over the salted surface and then it is sprinkled with oil; this is the well-known *Pa amb Tomàquet* of mainland Catalonia, about which Leopold Pomés has written one of the most humorous food books I have ever come across. ('One hundred metres away from where Catalan is spoken, bread and tomato come to an end', he says. He also reports the predictable results of a poll of 833,422 Catalan grandparents who were asked whether they had ever eaten (a) *pa amb tomàquet,* and (b) a lukewarm surmullet liver salad, perfumed with non-starched new potato.)

In Majorcan bars and restaurants they would top it with a slice of *jamón serrano* or cheese, with a few olives on the side. Then it becomes a first course, a light supper dish, or just *tapas* to have with beer or a glass of wine.

Unfortunately, not all bakeries make the distinctively flavoured *pan payes,* but a good alternative, available everywhere, is the circular hard-crusted *pan* (bread), as it is simply called; and with this one has the choice of either *sin sal,* without salt, or *con sal,* with salt. Like *pan payes,* it can be bought in a large or small size.

SOPES MALLORQUINAS DE VERDURA

| *Sopas mallorquinas* | Majorcan bread and |
| *de verdura* | vegetable dish |

In 1983 the Spanish magazine *Telva* organised a national cookery competition. This recipe, a Palma housewife's entry in the Majorcan regional finals, is a popular version of *sopas mallorquinas* for late winter and spring when the variety of vegetables required is easily available.

100 ml (3½ fl oz) olive oil	salt
4 or 5 large spring onions, including the green parts, chopped	200 g (7 oz) shelled peas
	1 small cauliflower
	500 g (1 lb) artichokes
3 cloves of garlic, chopped	meat stock or water
1 tbs finely chopped parsley	1 bunch fresh spinach, shredded
1 large ripe tomato, peeled and chopped	300 g (11 oz) *sopas mallorquinas*
1 heaped tsp mild paprika	

Heat the oil in a casserole and soften the spring onion and garlic, then add the parsley and tomato. When it has thickened, add the paprika and season with salt. Stir in the peas; the cauliflower, cut into small florets; and the artichokes, with the outer leaves removed to reveal the pale inner leaves, then cut in half and the hairy choke scooped out. Cover with good meat stock if you have it, otherwise with water, and bring to the boil. Simmer for 20 minutes, then add the spinach and cook for 5 minutes more.

Arrange the *sopas* in a heated earthenware *greixonera* or serving dish. Pour on the broth strained from the vegetables and leave for a couple of minutes to let the bread soak up the liquid. Finally, arrange the vegetables on top, sprinkle with good quality olive oil and serve with olives and raw radishes.

SOPES DE MATANCES

Sopas de matanzas   A bread, pork and cabbage dish

Originally a dish served at the annual *matanza de cerdo,* the domestic pig killing. The fact that excellent pork is now readily available has turned it into a popular item on restaurant menus. Indeed it was presented by the Restaurante Ca'n Mateu of Algaida at *La Mostra de Cuina Mallorquina* (the First Exhibition of Majorcan Cookery) in Palma in 1985.

This is a dish for late autumn or winter, and the quantities given serve 6.

400 g (14 oz) pork, cut from the leg (*carne magra*) sliced thinly and cut into squares of 2 cm (¾″)
200 ml (7 fl oz) olive oil
6 cloves garlic, peeled
150 g (5 oz) *setas* (wild mushrooms), sliced
2 onions, finely chopped
2 tbs mild paprika

300 g (11 oz) very ripe tomatoes, skinned and roughly chopped
1 small green cabbage (400 g/14 oz), shredded
1 tbsp finely chopped parsley
salt
150 g (5 oz) thinly sliced country bread (*sopas mallorquinas*)

Heat the olive oil in a *greixonera,* fry the garlic cloves until golden, then add the pieces of pork and continue to fry gently for a few minutes. Now add the mushrooms and onions. When the latter have softened, stir in the paprika and tomatoes and cook gently until a thickish sauce has formed. Add the cabbage and parsley and pour in enough water to cover. Season with salt and simmer for 30 minutes.

Finally, use a slotted spoon to remove the vegetables, add the *sopas* to the liquid, put the vegetables back on top and heat through. Dress with good olive oil and serve at once.

SOPA DE PA PER HIVERN

Sopa de pan para invierno   A winter bread dish

300 g (11 oz) pig's liver
2 heaped tbsp finely
  chopped parsley
8 peppercorns, ground
3 cloves, ground
200 g (7 oz) finely sliced
  country bread (*sopas*
  mallorquinas)

50 g (2 oz) hazelnuts,
  toasted and ground
700 ml (25 fl oz) meat stock
salt
ground cinnamon
10 g (3 ½ oz) grated
  Majoran cheese

Simmer the liver in a little water for 20 minutes, then let it cool, grate it roughly, and mix it with the parsley, pepper and cloves.

Spread the *sopas* out on a baking tray and crisp them briefly in the oven, letting them take colour but no more.

Put half the meat stock in a saucepan, whisk in the hazelnuts and simmer on a low heat for 5 minutes.

Meanwhile, in a *greixonera*, arrange a layer of the crisped *sopas*, then a layer of the liver mixture with a sprinkling of salt and cinnamon, then another layer of *sopas* ... and so on, finishing with a layer of *sopas*. Pour the simmering sauce over this and leave it on a low heat for just some seconds, while the bread absorbs all the stock. Then remove from the heat, pour on the rest of the stock, top with the grated cheese, and put in the hot oven until the cheese has melted and is bubbling and golden.

This dish can also be prepared in individual earthenware bowls.

PAN-CUIT

Sopa de ajo   Bread and garlic 'soup'

This is the Majorcan version of a dish which, in slightly different forms, is familiar throughout Spain, in the south of France, and in some other Mediterranean countries. The combination of bread, garlic, and olive oil is a basic one.

12 cloves garlic, peeled and
  lightly crushed
150 ml (5 fl oz) olive oil
1½ litre (36 fl oz) water
salt

3 tsp paprika
80 g (3 oz) stale *pan payes*
  or bread roll
3 eggs, beaten

Heat the oil in a pan and fry the garlic cloves until golden. Add the water, with a little salt and the paprika. Crumble in the stale bread. Bring to the boil and simmer for 10 minutes, when the bread and water should be well blended. Check the seasoning.

Remove the soup from the heat and quickly stir in the eggs, then serve at once in soup bowls.

Rice

Rice was brought to Spain by the Moors who invaded the Peninsula in 711 AD (and eventually Majorca in 902 AD), contributing at the same time their word for rice, *ar-roz,* to the Spanish vocabulary; it is *arroz* in Castilian and *arros* in Mallorquin. So its position as a basic food throughout the whole of Spain has a long history. The most popular rice in Majorca is the medium grain kind which is used in *paellas,* casseroles and soups, and is generally coloured with saffron. This kind is also used for rice puddings and rice based drinks.

Long grain rice is used mainly as a plain boiled rice to accompany other foods. A popular Majorcan practice is to serve it, cooked with a few whole garlic cloves, at the end of the meal to mop up any sauce left over from a meat casserole.

There are a number of dishes in Majorca, and indeed on the mainland, that are considered purely lunchtime dishes. Many of these are rice-based, for example the internationally known *paella,* of which there are many regional variations. It is a favourite choice for Sunday lunch. Indeed, if you find local people ordering *paella* in a restaurant in the evening, you can be sure that it is exceptionally good.

In Majorca it is normal for rice, or a rice-based dish, to be the first course, and tradition requires that it be accompanied by a small plate of fresh radishes and strips of raw red and green peppers, together with slices of lemon to squeeze over the rice: something not usually seen in restaurants in tourist areas.

SAFFRON, an important ingredient in many Majorcan rice dishes is best bought in pistil (or 'thread') form. Although it is expensive (even in Spain where the best saffron, that of Valencia, is produced), a little goes a long way and 6 pistils are enough to colour a *paella* or fish soup for 4 people.

Most restaurants and many domestic cooks nowadays use a

colour, which is also of course much cheaper. The use of *pimenton rojo* (the Spanish version of paprika popular in Majorcan cooking) with saffron gives a much more fashionable colour whilst retaining the authentic flavour.

To use saffron, pound the tiny pistils in a small pestle and mortar and add 3 or 4 tablespoons of hot water or some of the hot cooking liquid. Leave to infuse for a few minutes until the liquid is a bright orange colour. This is then strained into the rice dish at the appropriate moment.

ARROS DE PEIX

Arroz a la marinera   Fisherman's rice

This is just one of the many versions of a fish soup common in Mediterranean coastal cookery, made from various little fish trawled up with other catches and too small to be used in any other way. The fish are simmered in water and then discarded, rice or occasionally tiny pasta being cooked in the broth. This is roughly how the dish is served in Majorcan restaurants, and the recipe I give below corresponds to this method.

Note, however, that when the soup is made in a Majorcan home the fish are not allowed to disintegrate, but are saved to be eaten as a second course, with oil and vinegar. To be succesful in doing this, the cook needs some knowledge of the various species of fish which makes up *morralla,* the collective Spanish name for these soup fish. Those with firm flesh (e g scorpion fish, weevers) need to be cooked longer than the others; but care has to be taken not to let any disintegrate.

Alan Davidson's *Mediterranean Seafood* is an invaluable help for identifying the various fish, crustaceans and molluscs which may be met in Majorcan markets. The one fish he didn't have, our esteemed *raor* (p 121), has been snuck into the latest edition as a result of my telling him about it.

1 kg (2 ¼ lb) cleaned and scaled *morralla* (see above)	1 small cuttlefish or squid (125-150 g/4-5 oz)
6 tbsp olive oil	4 garlic cloves
1 onion	6 pistils saffron
1 large ripe tomato	1 tbsp roughly chopped parsley
1 heaped tsp paprika	1 tbsp peas, or chopped red pepper
1 tsp salt	
1 ½ litres (54 fl oz) water	100 g (3 ½ oz) medium grain rice

Scale the fish carefully, using a knife or a special scaling implement, and snip off the spikes and fins. Cut up and wash the fish. Heat 4 tablespoons of the olive oil in a saucepan and soften the roughly chopped onion and chopped tomato (there is no need to peel it) until a thick sauce has formed. Stir in the paprika and a teaspoon of salt, and the water. At the same time add all the fish and bring to the boil. Simmer for 15 minutes.

Meanwhile clean the cuttlefish or squid, removing eyes, beak, innards (including ink sac) and 'bone'. Cut the body into thin strips and the tentacles into small pieces. Heat 2 tablespoons of the olive oil in another large saucepan and fry the cuttlefish or squid carefully (it has a tendency to spit) for about 2 minutes. Remove from the heat.

Crush the saffron pistils and moisten with 3 or 4 tablespoons of the fish broth and leave to infuse. Pound the garlic and parsley together in a pestle and mortar.

Strain the fish broth through a fine sieve into the saucepan containing the cuttlefish, discarding fish and other remnants. Bring the broth to the boil and add the peas or red pepper and the rice. Simmer for 12 minutes, adding the strained saffron infusion, parsley and garlic 5 minutes before the end of the cooking time.

Leave to stand for 5 minutes and serve with slices of lemon and radishes on the side.

ARROS BRUT

Arroz brut   Hunter's rice

A filling and extremely popular winter dish which was originally made with hare, but is now usually prepared with a variety of meat and game. The difference between *arroz brut* and a *paella* is that *arroz brut* is more liquid and is traditionally cooked and served in a deep earthenware pot which resembles a soup tureen. Snails are frequently added to the dish and I have included them in this recipe, which is for 6 people.

300 g (11 oz) rabbit
200 g (7 oz) pork ribs
2 pigeons
3 thrushes or quails
5 tbsp olive oil
1 large onion, finely
  chopped
1 large ripe tomato,
  skinned and chopped
3 garlic cloves, chopped
2¼ litres (80 fl oz) water
150 g (5 oz) mange-tout
  peas
150 g (5 oz) *setas* (wild
  mushrooms)

2 large artichokes
6 saffron pistils
24 cooked snails with some
  of their cooking liquid
  (see p 166) (optional)
200 g (7 oz) medium grain
  rice
a small piece dried red
  chilli pepper
1 tbsp finely chopped
  parsley
¼ tsp ground cinnamon
¼ tsp ground cloves
salt and pepper

Cut the rabbit into small pieces and separate the pork ribs. Quarter the cleaned pigeons, thrushes or quails.

Heat the olive oil in a large saucepan (or earthenware pot) and in it brown the pieces of meat a few at a time. Remove and reserve each batch as they are done, with a slotted spoon. In the same oil soften the onion, then add the tomato and the garlic cloves. Simmer until a sauce has formed and then return all the meat to the saucepan. Pour on the water and bring to the boil. Season with salt and pepper and simmer for one hour.

Meanwhile, top and tail the mange-tout peas. Carefully clean the *setas,* cutting them in half if they are large. Trim the artichokes, removing the tough outer leaves, and cut each one in half. Remove the central hairy choke with a knife, then divide each half into four pieces. Drop these pieces into a bowl of cold water, with the juice of a lemon added to prevent discoloration, until ready for use.

At the end of the hour's cooking time, crush the saffron pistils in a mortar and pour on 4 tablespoons of the cooking liquid. Leave to infuse.

Add the mange-tout peas, *setas* and the drained and dried artichokes, together with the snails and a little of their cooking liquid, to the meat in the pan. Bring back to the boil and simmer for 5 minutes before adding the rice. Once the rice is added, quickly return to the boil and simmer for 20 minutes, uncovered. Grind the piece of chilli pepper and mix it with the parsley, ground cinnamon and cloves. About 10 minutes before the end of cooking time, add these and the strained saffron infusion to the saucepan. When the rice is cooked, leave the dish to stand for 2 minutes before serving in soup bowls with radishes and slices of lemon to squeeze onto the rice.

ARROS BRUT II

Arroz brut II   Hunter's rice II

A simpler, everyday version without small game birds or snails.

½ rabbit
½ chicken
200 g (7 oz) *carne magra,*
   pork cut from the leg
6 tbsp olive oil
1 onion, finely chopped
200 g (7 oz) ripe tomatoes,
   skinned and chopped
3 garlic cloves, chopped
1 tsp mild paprika

1½ litres (54 fl oz) water
salt and pepper
2 large artichokes
100 g (4 oz) medium grain
   rice
4 cloves
6 black peppercorns
a small piece cinnamon
a small piece dried chilli
   pepper

Have the butcher chop all the meat into small pieces. Fry these in batches with half the oil in a frying pan until browned.

In a large saucepan or earthenware casserole heat the remaining half of the oil and fry the onion until soft. Add the tomatoes and the garlic and leave to simmer for 10 minutes. When a thick sauce has formed, add the paprika and the water and bring to the boil. Add the fried pieces of meat and season with salt and pepper. Leave to simmer for one hour.

Trim the artichokes and cut into quarters, or smaller slices if you prefer, removing the hairy chokes. Add to the casserole with the rice. Return to the boil and simmer for 20 minues.

Crush in a pestle and mortar the cloves, peppercorns, cinnamon and chilli pepper and add to the *arroz brut* just before serving it in bowls (with radishes and slices of fresh peppers and lemons on the side).

PAELLA DE PEIX

Paella de pescado   Seafood paella

A *paella* takes its name from the metal pan in which it is cooked and served, a sort of two-handled frying pan which requires some special attentions. A new *paella* must first be rubbed with vinegar, and a little rice and water cooked in it, to remove the metallic taste. You then dry it well and rub it with oil to prevent it from rusting; and this oiling has to be repeated after every use of the pan.

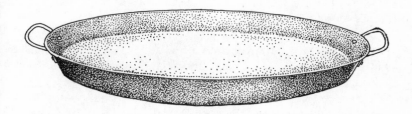

Paella pans come in various sizes, and the right size must be used for a specific number of people. Lourdes March, in her book *El Libro de la Paella y de Los Arroces,* recommends the following diameters:

    for 2-3 people: 30 cm/12"   for 10 people: 55 cm/22"
    for 4-5 people: 40 cm/16"   for 12 people: 60 cm/24"
    for 6-8 people: 50 cm/20"

Two general tips: when you are making a *paella,* the rice is never washed; and additional boiling water or stock must always be available to add to the rice if necessary.

The most popular *paella* in Spain is the Valencian version, combining meat and seafood, and this is what is served in many Majorcan restaurants; but Majorcans cooking at home often make an excellent *paella* featuring seafood only.

One Majorcan chef I know uses salt cod (*bacalao*) as the base for his *paella* — fine if you like salt cod. But it is more usual to use firm white fish such as hake or angler-fish.

In the recipe given here, which comes from the Restaurante Cova Rotja in Puerto de Andraitx, the fish used is *gató* (spotted dogfish).

for the fish stock, and the saffron infusion

5-6 tbsp olive oil

½ kg (1 lb 2 oz) *morralla* mixed small fish (p 66), cleaned and scaled

1 onion, roughly chopped

1 tomato, roughly chopped

1 litre (35 fl oz) water

salt

6 pistils saffron

Heat the olive oil in a large saucepan and fry the onion and tomato in it until the tomato has turned into a purée. Pour in the water and add the *morralla*, bring to the boil and leave to simmer for 20 minutes or until all the fish have disintegrated. Strain through a fine sieve, reserving the liquid only, and season this with salt to taste. You will need a few tablespoons of this stock for the saffron infusion, and 1 litre (36 fl oz) for the *paella*, with a little in reserve.

Crush the saffron pistils in a pestle and mortar, pour over them 3-4 tablespoons of the hot fish stock, and leave to infuse.

for the paella

450 g (1 lb) slices of dogfish

1 cuttlefish weighing about 175 g (6 oz)

200 ml (7 fl oz) olive oil

1 medium onion, very finely chopped

1 large ripe tomato, skinned and roughly chopped

1 small red pepper, finely diced

50 g (2 oz) shelled peas or finely sliced green beans

400 g (14 oz) medium grain rice

2 cloves garlic

1 tbsp roughly chopped parsley

salt

1 heaped tsp paprika

8 large uncooked prawns

8 large uncooked mussels

Clean the cuttlefish, removing innards, eyes, beak and 'bone'. Slice the body into thin strips and the tentacles into small pieces. Crush the garlic and parsley together in a mortar.

Heat the olive oil in a *paella* of 40 cm (16″) and fry the slices of dogfish in this until they are slightly browned. Remove and reserve them.

Now fry the pieces of cuttlefish in the same oil, adding the onion after a minute or so. When the onion has softened, add the tomato, red pepper, and peas (or beans), and continue cooking for a few minutes. Next, stir the paprika in thoroughly, and then the rice.

After the rice has cooked for just one minute or so, pour in ½ litre (18 fl oz) of boiling fish stock. Add the pieces of dogfish. Season with salt and with the garlic and parsley mixture, stir well with a wooden spoon and start to cook over a high flame.

As the fish stock begins to be absorbed by the rice, add the remaining ½ litre (18 fl oz) of it, together with the strained saffron infusion, without any further stirring. After 8 minutes of cooking over the high flame, lower the heat and cook the *paella* slowly for a further 10-12 minutes, still without any further stirring.

Meanwhile, either fry or boil the prawns (see p 144), and steam open the mussels (see p 151). You will, by the way, almost certainly have had to buy more than 8 mussels — but that is quite convenient, since you can steam them all open and serve the surplus ones as *tapas* with drinks before the *paella*.

When the final 10-12 minutes are up — at which point the rice will be cooked and nearly all the liquid absorbed — remove the *paella* from the heat and leave it to stand for 5 minutes.

Finally, arrange the mussels in their shells and the prawns on top of the *paella* and serve it with slices of lemon, strips of red and green peppers and radishes on the side.

ARROS EN EL FORN

Arroz al horno a la mallorquina   Baked Majorcan rice

One of those robust, earthy Majorcan dishes, which offers another way of preparing rice, this time baking it in the oven in a flat-bottomed glazed circular earthenware dish, about 6 cm (2¼″) deep. These dishes come in various sizes and are easily available and inexpensive in Majorca. The size required for this recipe is the one measuring 35 cm (14″), which is sufficient for 6 people. If you wish to halve the recipe, a dish measuring 25 cm (10″) will be right, and this is the size I find most useful.

100 g (3½ oz) *sobrasada,*
  skinned and in thick slices
100 g (3½ oz) cooked
  chickpeas
2 medium potatoes
3 medium tomatoes
1 whole head garlic

100 ml (3½ fl oz) olive oil
¾ litre (27 fl oz) meat
  stock
400 g (14 oz) medium
  grain rice
salt and pepper

Peel the potatoes and cut into small dice. Cut two of the tomatoes in half and skin the third, chopping it roughly. Separate the cloves from the head of garlic and crush each clove slightly without peeling it. Preheat the oven to 250°C (400°F/gas mark 6).

Heat the olive oil in the earthenware dish and fry the whole garlic cloves with the diced potato until they are just beginning to take colour. Add the tomato halves and fry them for just a few seconds, then add the chopped tomato, the chickpeas and the slices of *sobrasada.* Next, stir in the rice and, once it is well mixed in, pour on the boiling stock. When the liquid comes back to the boil, season with salt and pepper and place the dish in the oven for 15 to 18 minutes, when the rice should be cooked and all the liquid absorbed.

Serve at once in the same dish.

Pasta

Pasta, reflecting neighbourly influences, has become very popular in Majorca. The dried packet varieties such as spaghetti, fettucine, macaroni, canneloni, lasagne, vermicelli, and all the tiny shaped pastas are available everywhere. Palma, the capital, now boasts La Casa Italiana, a fresh pasta shop in calle de Anibal near the Santa Catalina market, with a small branch in calle Plateria, near Plaza Mayor.

Vermicelli and the tiny shaped pastas are now often added to soups instead of rice. Spaghetti bolognese appears on many Majorcan restaurant menus, not just in the tourist areas. Macaroni, with a tomato and meat sauce, is a regular first course both in the home and in the many *restaurantes economicos* (which serve, at lunch-time, well-cooked three-course meals with bread and wine or water at a very low price).

Canneloni is probably the best loved pasta, often made for special occasions. I remember that at a Christmas Day lunch given by my friend Baltazar's family, canneloni was served as the first course, stuffed with squid, in a rich bechamel sauce.

Cooking pasta correctly is important. It should be cooked until just slightly resistant to the bite (the Italian *al dente*). For 100 g (4 oz) of pasta you need about 1½ litre (54 fl oz) of boiling salted water; and you must stir with a wooden spoon to prevent any sticking to the bottom of the saucepan or 'clumping' of the pasta in the water. Fresh pasta should only need 3 or 4 minutes' cooking; but dried packet spaghetti or fettucine requires 10 to 15 minutes, and macaroni needs 20.

FIDEUS AMB AGULLES

Fideos con agujas   Vermicelli with gar-fish

The gar-fish has a slight greenish tinge to its scales, and its backbone turns bright green when it is cooked. It is a delicious fish, with no fiddly little bones, and is most plentiful in late summer and autumn. If you wish to make the dish when gar-fish is not to be had, and don't mind buying something a little more expensive, you could try using red mullet (cooked whole); or pieces of skate; or steaks of *serviola* (amberjack, p 124).

My recipe gives a wide range for the amount of vermicelli; this must depend on appetite.

½ kg (1 lb) gar-fish
100-200 g (3-7 oz) vermicelli
100 ml (3 ½ fl oz) olive
    oil
1 onion, finely chopped
1 large ripe tomato,
    skinned and chopped

2 garlic cloves, peeled
1 large potato, peeled
    and cubed
100 g (3 ½ oz) shelled
    peas
salt and pepper
1 tbsp chopped parsley

Clean and skin the gar-fish and cut it into pieces. Heat the oil in a large saucepan and soften the onion in it, then add the tomato and one of the garlic cloves, roughly chopped. Simmer until this has become a thickish sauce, then pour in 1 litre (36 fl oz) of water, bring to the boil, add the potato and peas, and simmer for 5-10 minutes more. When the potato is almost cooked, add the vermicelli and the pieces of fish, season and leave to go on cooking for a further 10 minutes.

Crush the second garlic clove with the parsley in a mortar, moisten it with a little of the cooking liquid and stir it into the main mixture just before serving.

Serve with olives and pickled samphire (*hinojo marino*), which is available in most markets.

CANELONS FARCIT DE CARN

Canalones rellenos de carne   Canneloni stuffed with meat

In Spain, pasta to make canneloni is commonly sold in flat sheets, rather than as tubes. You have to cook these in boiling salted water for 10 to 15 minutes before using them. (However, you may come across a new kind which only needs a couple of hours soaking in water to be ready for use.)

16 sheets of pasta for
  canneloni (see above)
3 tbsp olive oil
1 onion, finely chopped
1 large ripe tomato,
  skinned and chopped
¼ chicken, in one piece

1 thick slice *tocino*
  or pork fat
1 lamb steak, from the leg
100 ml (3 ½ fl oz) dry
  white wine
salt and pepper
grated cheese

Heat the oil in a large saucepan and fry the onion in it until lightly coloured. Add the tomato and continue to cook gently for about 10 minutes, until you have a thick sauce. Then turn the heat up high and put in the chicken, *tocino* and lamb, turning each piece so that it is well coated with the sauce. Pour on the wine, and season generously. Cover the pan and simmer until the meat is cooked.

Remove all the meat from the pan, cut it off the bone, and chop it very finely with a sharp knife or mince it in a mincer. Then return it to the pan and simmer until the mixture thickens. It is to be your stuffing.

Meanwhile, you have prepared your sheets of pasta (see above). Put a spoonful of the stuffing on each sheet and roll it up to form a tube. Arrange the tubes side by side in an ovenproof dish, cover with bechamel sauce (recipe overleaf), and top with grated cheese*. Bake in a moderate oven (180°C/355°F/gas mark 4) for half an hour.

*The best known Balearic cheese comes from the island of Minorca. Known as Mahon cheese, it is available in various stages of maturity. The very mature *Mahones viejo* has a sharp, salty flavour and a hard texture not unlike that of Parmesan.

SALSA BECHAMEL

Salsa bechamel   Bechamel sauce

¾ litre (27 fl oz) milk   2 egg yolks, beaten
1 onion stuck with 2 cloves   salt and white pepper
50 g (2 oz) lard   grated nutmeg
50 g (2 oz) flour

Put the milk and the onion into a saucepan and bring to the boil
as slowly as possible. Melt the lard in another pan and stir the
flour into it until well blended.

Remove the onion from the milk and whisk the milk into the
flour and lard mixture over a low heat. When the sauce has
thickened, simmer for 5 minutes, continuing to stir. Remove
from the heat and whisk in the beaten egg yolks. Finally, season
with the salt and white pepper and grated nutmeg.

CANELONS FARCITS DE CALAMARS

Canalones rellenos   Canneloni stuffed
de calamares   with squid

16 sheets of pasta for   *for the stuffing*
    making canneloni   250 g (9 oz) cleaned squid
    (see p 77)   1 clove of garlic
for the sofrito   some fresh parsley
2 tbsp olive oil   ¼ onion, roughly chopped
1 onion, finely chopped   a little milk
2 cloves of garlic, peeled   1 tbsp fresh breadcrumbs
    and roughly chopped   1 egg yolk
1 tbsp chopped parsley   a little olive oil
1 large tomato, peeled and   salt and pepper
    chopped   *for the sauce*
¾ litre (27 fl oz) water   2 tbsp lard or olive oil
salt and pepper   1 onion, finely chopped
                               1 tbsp diced serrano ham
                               2 tbsp flour
                               2 egg yolks
                               salt and white pepper

First make the *sofrito*. Heat the oil in a saucepan, add the onion and garlic, and fry gently until the onion is soft. Stir in the parsley and tomato and simmer for about 10 minutes, until the mixture has thickened.

Next, add the water and seasoning, bring to the boil and put in the squid, preferably whole. Simmer for 15 minutes or until the squid is cooked, then remove it from the liquid, chop it finely and place it in a mixing bowl. Strain the liquid and reserve it for use when making the sauce.

Now you can prepare the stuffing. In a mortar, pound the garlic clove with the parsley and onion. Moisten with a little milk, then stir the mixture into the squid in the mixing bowl. Add the breadcrumbs; then the egg yolk, beaten with a little olive oil; and lastly the seasoning.

Meanwhile you have boiled the pieces of pasta for 10 to 15 minutes in plenty of salted water. Drain them, put a spoonful of the stuffing on each piece, roll them up to form tubes, and arrange them side by side in an ovenproof dish.

To prepare the sauce, melt the lard or heat the oil in a saucepan and fry the onion until golden. Add the ham and stir in the flour. Over a low heat, whisk in the strained cooking liquid, and continue to stir until a thick sauce has formed. Whisk in the beaten egg yolks and season with salt and white pepper.

Pour the sauce over the stuffed canneloni and bake them for half an hour in a moderate oven (180°C/355°F/gas mark 4).

If you prefer, you need not make the special sauce provided for in this recipe, but could use bechamel sauce (see the preceding page) instead.

MACARRONS

Macarrones   Macaroni

The standard Majorcan macaroni dish consists of boiled macaroni tossed in a tomato-based bolognese-style sauce. The recipe I give here is more interesting, and very simple to prepare.

250 g (9 oz) macaroni
2 tbsp olive oil
1 medium onion, finely
  chopped
2 large ripe tomatoes,
  peeled and roughly
  chopped
½ tsp dried oregano

½ tsp dried mint
1 bay leaf
125 ml (4½ fl oz) good
  meat stock
2 heaped tbsp freshly
  chopped parsley
salt and pepper

Boil the macaroni in salted water until cooked, then drain it. Heat the oil in a saucepan and soften the onion in this, then add the tomatoes, oregano, mint and bay leaf. Simmer for 5 minutes, then pour in the meat stock, season with salt and pepper, and simmer for 5 minutes more. Finally, stir in the cooked macaroni and the parsley, heat through and serve.

Eggs

Eggs bought from the weekly market stalls or village *colmados* will invariably be free-range and very fresh. Since these eggs are sold loose, not pre-packed in cartons as in supermarkets, there is no compulsion to buy them in units of half dozen; indeed it is sometimes possible to buy just one egg, though pricing is usually done by the half dozen.

Besides being a basic ingredient in many Majorcan recipes, eggs are a common garnish. Either hard-boiled or in the form of thinly sliced ribbons of *tortilla*, they adorn many meat and vegetable dishes.

OUS A LA SOLLERICA

Huevos a la Sollerica   Eggs, Soller style

Soller is a town in Majorca. You may find this dish referred to on menus by the alternative name *Huevos a la mallorquina*.

200 g (7 oz) peas	8 slices *sobrasada,* skinned
3 carrots, sliced	olive oil for frying
2 large leeks, sliced	8 eggs
250 ml (9 fl oz) meat stock	salt and pepper

Cook the peas, carrots and leeks in the stock. Then use a blender or vegetable mill to make them into a thin purée. Sieve this and keep it warm.

Fry the slices of *sobrasada* in a little olive oil, then place them in an ovenproof serving dish. Fry the eggs in the same oil, then put them on top of the *sobrasada*. Cover the eggs with the vegetable purée and leave the dish in a hot oven for 5 minutes before serving it.

TRUITA MALLORQUINA

Tortilla mallorquina   Majorcan omelette

Another linguistic snare for tourists. *Truita* doesn't mean trout, but is the Catalan name for omelette.

A Spanish *tortilla* is not at all like the sort of omelette familiar in France and Britain. It is thicker and round and, because cooked on both sides, firm and well set. It can be served hot or cold and in either case is cut into wedges like a cake.

The *Tortilla espanola,* which is the standard version, has potato in it. It is very popular in Majorca, as well as on the mainland. It appears in suitably small pieces at *tapas* bars and at *fiestas,* and is often served as a supper dish.

This *Tortilla mallorquina* differs in one respect only: the addition of *sobrasada.*

8 slices *sobrasada,* peeled	8 eggs
½ kg (1 lb) potatoes,	salt and pepper
peeled and cut into chips	¼ litre (9 fl oz) olive oil

In a little of the olive oil quickly fry the slices of *sobrasada* on both sides, remove and keep warm. Add the rest of the olive oil to the frying pan and fry the chipped potatoes until soft. Now carefully pour most of the oil out of the frying-pan and add the well seasoned, beaten eggs. Stir continuously over a medium heat to incorporate the thickening egg mixture with the potatoes. Turn the heat down low, add the slices of *sobrasada* and cook until set, shaking the pan occasionally.

Remove the frying-pan from the heat, place a dinner plate over it and turn out the *tortilla*. Return the frying-pan to the heat and slide the *tortilla,* uncooked side down, back into the pan. Cook quickly, shaking the pan, for a minute or so to let the *tortilla* set. Turn onto a serving plate with the side showing the *sobrasada* slices uppermost, and serve hot or cold, cut into wedges.

TRUITA DE ESPARRECS BORDS

Tortilla de esparragos   Wild asparagus
silvestre   omelette

Local wild asparagus can be bought in bunches from either the Olivar or the Santa Catalina Market in Palma, from the end of January to the end of April — but it is more fun to go and look for your own in the hedgerows and stone walls bordering fields. The wispy asparagus spears grow out of the centre of very thorny, bushy clumps and to extract them without tearing your hands to shreds is an art. Wild asparagus conveniently comes into season just as the wild mushrooms are finishing and because asparagus-gathering is so popular, finding an area which has remained unpicked is also an art.

Wild asparagus is slightly bitter, but the flavour combines remarkably well with eggs, especially in a *tortilla* which, in this case, should be served hot. They look good made up as individual *tortilla* using a small frying-pan, but can also be made as the traditional cake and cut into wedges. For one person I use a good handful of asparagus and three eggs, though I cut this down to two eggs each if making a large one for four people.

Use only the wheat-like tips of the asparagus and after washing gently, fry them for about 5 minutes in some virgin olive oil in an appropriate frying-pan. Drain off the excess oil and stir in the beaten eggs seasoned with salt and pepper. Continue stirring over a medium heat to combine the thickening egg mixture with the asparagus spears, then turn the heat down and cook gently until firm, shaking the pan occasionally.

Turn the *tortilla* to let the uncooked side set and then serve.

JONQUILLO

Chanquete   'Transparent goby' fritters

There are many species of goby in the Mediterranean. The particular one used in this recipe is very small and has a 'transparent' body, which accounts for its rather unwieldy English name.

These little gobies are very popular throughout Spain. In Majorca, they are available between December and June, when heaps of them, an unattractive glutinous mass dotted with tiny black eyes, can be seen in the markets and shops. The most common way of serving them is to fry them in batter, as a *tapa*, but they also make a good first course if combined with eggs as in this recipe.

200 g (7 oz) transparent
  gobies
4 tbsp flour
2 eggs
1 tbsp finely chopped
  parsley

2 garlic cloves, finely
  chopped
salt and pepper
oil for frying

Place the gobies in a sieve and wash them under cold running water. Drain and dry on kitchen paper.

Make a stiff batter by putting the flour into a bowl and making a well in the centre. Break in the eggs and beat with a wooden spoon until the eggs and flour are blended together smoothly. Stir in the parsley and the garlic, season, and mix the transparent gobies in gently. Heat a pan of oil and drop in the mixture by the spoonful. Fry, turning occasionally, until golden brown all over. Serve hot with lemon wedges.

Savoury Pies and Pastries

Savoury pastries were introduced into Spain by the Moors; and they are still, of course, a feature of Middle Eastern and North African cookery. Anyone travelling between Spain and, say, Morocco or Syria is bound to be struck by this point of resemblance as well as by others. These savoury pastries may also be recognized elsewhere, in countries where the culinary influence of Spain has been at work, for example many in Central and South America and, via that continent, the Philippines.

In Majorca, half moon shapes, small 'pots', flat tarts and large pies have become common, filled with meat or vegetables. They can be bought from a baker or made at home. Served hot or cold, they make a good first course. Majorcans prefer most of them cold.

The drawing below shows Majorcan *empanadas*.

PANADES D'ANYELL LLISES

Empanadas de cordero lisas   Savoury lamb pies

Panades containing lamb are customarily made by Majorcan families at Easter, though they are now available all year round from bakeries, filled not only with lamb but also fish and peas. They are generally referred to by their Castilian name *empanada,* but it is the homemade Easter lamb *panades* that are the best. In the past, any left over from Easter were kept until the following Sunday when people went into the country to eat them. This old custom is kept up at Bellver Castle near Palma where the town council organises entertainment. *Pancaritat,* as the day is known, is now also celebrated in other areas on different days during Easter Week.

Another version of *empanadas* is common, made with sweetened pastry; the origins of the dish are Moorish. Even today sweetened meat pies can be found in Moroccan cooking.

This recipe makes about a dozen small pies.

for the pastry:
500 g (1 lb) plain flour, sifted
75 g (2½ oz) lard
125 ml (4½ fl oz) olive oil
juice of one orange
125 ml (4½ fl oz) water
pinch of salt

for the filling:
½ kg (1 lb) boned shoulder of lamb, cut into bite-sized pieces
200 g (7 oz) *sobrasada,* skinned and cut into slices
100 g (3½ oz) fresh *tocino* or pork fat, diced
juice of one lemon
salt and pepper

Marinate the lamb for a couple of hours in the lemon juice, salt and pepper.

Make the pastry as in the recipe on page 90, but notice that no egg is necessary.

Let it rest for an hour or two. The dough should be stiff enough to hold its shape without a mould. To form the pies, take egg-sized balls of dough, hollow them out with your fingers and shape them into small pots by straightening up the sides.

Place a few pieces of *tocino* in the bottom, then some of the lamb and on top a piece of *sobrasada*. Cover each pot with a round lid of dough shaped with the flat of your hand.

Pinch and fold over the overlapping edges of each lid, sealing well, and then pinch a decorative pattern on the sealed edge. Bake at 200°C (390°F/gas mark 5) for 30-40 minutes until the pastry is a warm golden colour. Eat warm or cold.

Dough for COCAS

250 g (9 oz) plain flour
135 ml (5 fl oz) water
15 g (½ oz) fresh yeast
1 tbsp olive oil

25 g (1 oz) lard, cut into
small pieces
salt

Warm the water and dissolve the yeast in it, then stir in the lard and finally the oil. Leave for about 15 minutes in a warm place until frothy. Warm the flour and sift it with a pinch of salt into a bowl. Make a well in the centre and pour in the yeast mixture. Knead well until the dough forms a ball and leaves the sides of the bowl cleanly. Cover with a cloth or cling film and leave in a warm place until the dough has doubled in size. Knock down the risen dough and knead well.

Traditionally, *cocas* were baked in circular baking trays about 1 cm (½ ") deep, but now bakers usually make large rectangular ones for easier portioning, and use a shortcrust pastry base, which, though lighter, is not so delicious. Both circular and square baking trays of varying size are obtainable everywhere.

This amount of dough will line a circular, fluted baking tray of 34 cm (14"), sufficient for 8 people. Grease the baking tray and press in the dough to fit it evenly. The *coca* is now ready to be covered with vegetables, meat or fish and baked as required.

COCA AMB LLOM DE PORC I PEBRES

Coca con lomo de cerdo
y pimientos tostados

Majorcan pie with pork loin
and peppers

1 kg (2 ¼ lb) mixed red
and green peppers
8 slices loin of pork
2 tbsp finely chopped
parsley

4 garlic cloves, finely
chopped
olive oil
salt

You will need a circular baking tray, 34 cm (14″) in diameter, lined with prepared *coca* dough (p 87).

Grill or bake the peppers until the skins blacken and blister. Plunge into cold water, peel off the papery outer skin, remove the seeds, cut the flesh into quarters and mix with the sliced pork, parsley, garlic and salt in a bowl. Moisten with olive oil.

Arrange this mixture on top of the dough, making sure you put the pork slices, cut into small pieces, in such a way that when the *coca* is cut, each piece will have a slice of pork. Bake in a pre-heated moderate oven (180°C/355°F/gas mark 4) for 45 minutes. Remove from the oven, sprinkle with olive oil and serve warm or cold.

COCA DE TREMPO

Torta con verduras de verano	Summer vegetable tart
3 large green peppers, cut into small pieces	1 clove of garlic, finely chopped
2 white onions, halved and thinly sliced	1 tbsp chopped parsley
3 ripe tomatoes	½ tbsp mild paprika
400 g/14 oz in all), sliced thinly	salt
	olive oil

You will need a circular baking tray, 43 cm (14″) in diameter, lined with prepared *coca* dough (p 87).

Mix the peppers, onions, tomatoes, garlic, parsley and paprika, and season with salt. Spread this vegetable mixture on top of the dough, sprinkle olive oil over it, and bake in a pre-heated moderate oven (180°C/335°F/gas mark 4) for 40 minutes, until the dough has risen and is cooked.

After removing the dish from the oven, sprinkle a little more olive oil over the top. Serve warm or cold.

If you were to substitute ½ kg (1 lb) of shredded Swiss chard or spinach for the peppers, the pie would become a *Coca de verdura*.

COCARROIS

Pastelitos de espinacas,   Vegetable pasties with spinach,
pasas y piñones   pine nuts and raisins

The *cocarrois* sold in bakers' shops — shaped rather like Cornish pasties — usually just contain Swiss chard, pine nuts and raisins but a chance decision to call in and say goodbye to Baltazar's mother when I was making a short trip to England resulted in my tasting this recipe. There she was in the kitchen making up a batch of *cocarrois* which included miniature cauliflower florets. Her family had always made *cocarrois* this way when cauliflowers were in season. When they are out of season, one makes do without them, just shredding a few extra Swiss chard leaves to compensate.

Cocarrois are probably a local version of a Moorish pastry which would have used spinach. The Arabs introduced spinach to Europe, and a similar recipe is popular in Arab cookery today.

for the pastry
500 g (1 lb) flour
75 g (2½ oz) lard
125 ml (4½ fl oz) olive oil
juice of one orange
1 beaten egg
125 ml (4½ fl oz) water
salt

for the filling
1 bunch Swiss chard
   (about 5 big leaves)
½ small cauliflower, in
   tiny florets
1 tbsp pine nuts
1 tbsp whole raisins
1 tsp mild paprika
salt

First, make the pastry. Sift the flour and a pinch of salt into a bowl and rub in the lard. Make a hollow in the centre of the flour and pour in the olive oil, orange juice and water. Mix this in roughly before adding the beaten egg. Knead until a smooth dough is formed but avoid handling excessively or the finished pastry will be hard. Roll out on a floured surface, not too thinly, and cut into rounds, 12 cm (5″) in diameter. This makes about 12 pies.

To make the filling, wash and finely shred the Swiss chard, after discarding the thick stems. Mix the chard with the cauliflower florets, the pine nuts, raisins, salt and paprika. Place a spoonful of the mixture on top of each pastry circle, dampen the edges and bring the two sides together, at the top, sealing well. Pinch a decoration along the sealed edge. Bake at 200°C (390°F/gas mark 5) for 30-35 minutes. Serve warm or cold.

DUQUESES DE PEIX

Duquesas de pescado   Fish pies

Duquesas are a version of *empanadas* and are a good way of using up leftovers, especially chicken, white fish or tuna. This recipe makes 8 pies.

for the pastry
250 g (9 oz) plain flour, sifted
40 g (1 ½ oz) lard
1 tbsp olive oil
juice of one small orange
1 beaten egg
pinch of salt
for the filling
2 tbsp olive oil
1 tbsp lard
2 tbsp water

1 small onion finely chopped
2 tbsp flour
¼ litre (9 fl oz) milk
1 egg yolk
1 hard-boiled egg, chopped
2 tbsp chopped parsley
2 tbsp cooked, chopped spinach or Swiss chard
200 g (7 oz) cooked white fish flaked
salt and pepper

Make the pastry in the same way as the previous recipe.

Heat the oil, lard and water together until the lard has melted and fry the onion until it is a light golden colour. Stir in the flour and, away from the heat, whisk in the milk. Place the pan over a low heat and stir continuously until the mixture thickens. Remove from the heat and add the beaten egg yolk. When that is incorporated, stir in the hard-boiled egg, parsley, spinach and fish. Season well.

Form the dough into small pots by taking large egg-sized balls of the dough and hollowing them out with your fingers, then shaping them into small pots by straightening up the sides. Fill them with the mixture and bake in a pre-heated oven at 200°C (390°F/gas mark 5) for 30-35 minutes. Serve warm or cold.

Pulses

Dried pulses (*cuinats* in Mallorquin) have a high protein value and were in past centuries a boon to peasants who could not often afford meat. Indeed they still are in some places; and many recipes are still current in all regions of Spain for dried beans, chickpeas and lentils.

In Majorca, many of these dried pulse dishes are just household improvisations in which the pulses are combined with fresh vegetables, stock bones or offal according to season and availability. However, a few 'classic' dishes have emerged which are prepared in a more or less uniform manner throughout the island.

All kinds of dried pulses can be found everywhere, either pre-packed or loose in sacks. These have to be soaked overnight before use. Bottled pulses (mainly chickpeas, lentils and haricot beans) of excellent quality, ready cooked, are also easy to obtain, and do not of course need a soaking, but can just be added to the appropriate dishes near the end of the cooking time.

The recipes in this chapter are a mixture: some for dried pulses, some for fresh ones.

ESCUDELLA

Escudella   Dried haricot bean soup

This provides a filling winter soup for 6 people.

100 g (3 ½ oz) dried
  haricot beans
100 g (3 ½ oz) dried pinto
  beans
200 g (7 oz) green lentils
2 or 3 pieces of ham bone
150 g (5 oz) *tocino* (pork fat)
2 large potatoes, peeled
  and diced
200 g (7 oz) carrots, peeled
  and diced

200 g (7 oz) fresh green
  beans, sliced
a few handfuls of finely
  shredded green cabbage
2 tbsp olive oil
1 medium onion, finely
  chopped
1 large ripe tomato, peeled
  and chopped
2 garlic cloves, finely
  chopped
salt and pepper

After soaking all the beans and the lentils overnight, drain them and put them in a saucepan with the ham bones and *tocino*. Cover them with water, bring to the boil, then simmer until the beans are cooked. Now remove the ham bones and *tocino,* and add the potatoes, carrots, green beans and cabbage. Bring back to the boil and simmer for 20 to 30 minutes until everything is cooked sufficiently.

Meanwhile, heat the oil in a pan and soften the onion in it. Then add the tomato and garlic, and cook gently for 10 minutes, when a thick sauce should have formed.

Add this sauce to the vegetable mixture and simmer it all for another 10 minutes, then adjust the seasoning (add pepper, but salt may not be needed as the ham bones and *tocino* are quite salty), and serve.

The *tocino* can be diced and added to the soup before serving, if you wish.

ESCUDELLA FRESCA

Escudella fresca   Fresh vegetable and bean soup

This is another filling soup, but not a winter one. It is to be served on cold days in autumn and spring when the necessary fresh green beans are available.

2 pig's trotters, split, or 2 or 3 pieces of ham bone
1 large potato, peeled and diced
200 g (7 oz) pumpkin, peeled and diced
200 g (7 oz) green beans sliced
400 g (14 oz) mixture of any of the following:
  fresh chickpeas
  fresh butterbeans
  fresh haricot beans
  fresh pinto beans

2 tbsp olive oil
1 medium onion, finely chopped
1 large ripe tomato, finely chopped
2 garlic cloves, chopped
50 g (2 oz) *sobrasada,* sliced
50 g (2 oz) *butifarra,* sliced
salt and pepper

Singe off any hairs from the trotters, cover them with cold water in a saucepan, bring to the boil, and simmer briskly for 10 minutes. Drain and rinse the trotters. Clean the saucepan and put them back in it with fresh water, then simmer for an hour. (If you are using ham bones, just cover them with water in a saucepan, bring to the boil and simmer for an hour.)

Now add the potato, pumpkin, fresh green beans, and whatever other fresh legumes you have chosen. Simmer for about 30 minutes.

Meanwhile, make a *sofrito* by heating the oil, softening the onion in it, adding the tomato and garlic, and cooking gently for about 10 minutes, when it should have become a thick sauce. Add this to the vegetables. (You may at this stage remove the trotters or bones. If you have used trotters, these can be cut up and put back in the soup, if desired.) Stir in the *sobrasada* and *butifarra,* adjust the seasoning, simmer for 10 minutes and serve.

LLENTILLES CUINADES

Potaje de lentejas   Lentil soup

300 g (10 oz) green lentils
1 large onion, finely
  chopped
125 ml (4½ fl oz) olive
  oil
1 large ripe tomato, peeled
  and chopped

1 head of garlic, unpeeled
1 bay leaf
2 potatoes, peeled and
  diced
salt
wine vinegar

Having soaked the lentils overnight, drain them, put them in a pan, cover them with water, bring to the boil and simmer for 45 minutes to an hour, until they are cooked.

Make a *sofrito* by frying the onion in the oil until it is soft, adding the tomato and cooking gently for about 10 minutes until the mixture has thickened. Drain the lentils, clean their pan, and return them to it with the *sofrito,* the whole head of garlic, bay leaf, and potatoes. Season with salt and just cover with cold water. Simmer slowly for half an hour, adding a little more water if the soup becomes too thick.

Remove the head of garlic and the bay leaf, and serve very hot with a sprinkling of wine vinegar.

CUIRONS ESCALDINS

Garbanzos 'escaldins'   Chickpea stew

When you soak the chickpeas overnight, put in a pinch of bicarbonate of soda.

400 g (14 oz) dried
  chickpeas, (see above)
4 tbsp olive oil
3 cloves of garlic, peeled
  and chopped

1 large onion, finely
  chopped
1 large tomato, peeled
  and chopped
1 *butifarron,* sliced
a piece of *longaniza*

Rinse the soaked chickpeas and place in a saucepan, cover with cold water and bring to the boil. Simmer for about 1½ hours until the chickpeas are tender. Heat the olive oil in a *greixonera,* soften the onion and add the garlic and tomato. When a thick sauce has formed, stir in the cooked chickpeas, the *butifarron* and *longaniza.* Heat through. Finally, season with plenty of freshly ground black pepper and salt.

FAVA PELADA

Habas peladas   Dried broad bean stew

Fava is the Mallorquin for broad beans. This hearty winter soup requires peeled, dried broad beans, *fava pelada.* They are generally available wherever dried pulses are sold loose; at market stalls and certain *colmados* (grocers). Whole dried broad beans can also be used; their tough outer skin will slip off quite easily after soaking.

250 g (9 oz) dried, peeled
broad beans, soaked
overnight
1 large, split pig's trotter,
or ear; or pork ribs,
chopped into pieces
2 tbsp olive oil

1 large onion, finely
chopped
250 g (9 oz) potatoes,
peeled and diced
250 g (9 oz) white cabbage,
finely shredded
salt and pepper

If using trotters or the ear, singe off any hairs and simmer in water for 10 minutes. Drain and rinse in cold water and cut the ear into pieces or the trotter into four.

Soften the onion in the oil; add the drained beans and the trotter, ear or the pork ribs. Cover with cold water and simmer for an hour or until the beans are tender. Add the diced potato and shredded cabbage and continue to simmer for a further hour; the beans should form a thick purée with the potatoes. Season with salt and pepper and serve.

MONJETAS SEQUES ESTOFADES

Judias secas estofadas   Dried haricot bean stew

400 g (14 oz) dried haricot   1 bay leaf
  beans, soaked overnight   1 tsp mild paprika
5 cloves of garlic, peeled   a few pieces of marrow bone
1 onion, finely chopped   2 tbsp olive oil
a few sprigs of parsley   salt and pepper
a sprig of thyme

Drain the soaked beans and put them in a saucepan with all the
other ingredients except for oil, salt and pepper. (The parsley,
thyme and bay leaf can be tied together or put in a muslin bag
to make their subsequent removal easy.) Cover with cold water,
bring slowly to the boil, then cover and leave barely simmering
for 4 hours. The beans must cook very slowly. Add a little cold
water at intervals, to slow down the cooking.

When the beans are cooked, remove the marrow bones and
herbs. Take out a quarter of the beans and make them into a
purée. Return this to the pan, season, stir in the olive oil and
serve.

FAVES TENDRES OFEGADES

Habas tiernas 'ofegades'   Broad bean hotpot

1 ½ kg (3 ½ lb) young   a few small sprigs of mint
  broad beans in pods   2 large spring onions,
1 tbsp lard   finely sliced including
1 tbsp olive oil   the green parts
¼ litre (9 fl oz) water   2 *butifarrones,* sliced
                                     salt and pepper

Pod the beans. Then, in a *greixonera* (earthenware casserole), heat
the lard, olive oil and water to boiling point. Add the beans,
sprigs of mint, spring onions and *butifarrones.* Cook, uncovered,
on a low heat until the water has evaporated and the beans are
sizzling in the fat.

Season and serve with cooked young artichokes cut into quarters, and fresh Majorcan country bread. Or use as a side dish with plainly cooked meat or poultry.

PESOLS AMB AMETLLES

Guisantes con almendras   Peas with almonds

March to June are best for fresh peas. Although they are available again in the autumn, they tend to be very expensive.

1 kg (2 ¼ lb) peas
1 onion, finely chopped
1 ripe tomato, about 200 g
  (7 oz), peeled and
  chopped
1 bay leaf
1 tsp flour

meat stock (about ¼ litre,
  9 fl oz)
50 g (2 oz) peeled and
  toasted almonds
2 cloves garlic
fresh parsley
olive oil

Heat some oil in a casserole and fry the onion until soft. Add the tomato and bay leaf and cook slowly for 5 minutes.

Shell the peas and add them to the casserole. Stir in the flour, meat stock and some salt and pepper. Bring to the boil and simmer slowly for 15 minutes.

Meanwhile, prepare a *picada* by crushing the almonds in a mortar with the garlic, some roughly chopped parsley and a few drops of olive oil. Pound until the garlic is well incorporated with the almonds and parsley and stir in the casserole. Serve at once.

ESCUDELLA DE FAVES TENDRES

Escudella de habas tiernas   Broad bean stew

¼ litre (9 fl oz) meat stock
2 ½ kg (5 ½ lb) broad
  beans
50 g (2 oz) *jamón serrano,*
  diced small

¼ tsp dried marjoram
¼ tsp dried mint
2 *butifarrones,* sliced
50 g (2 oz) *sobrasada* in
  pieces

Bring the stock to the boil in an earthenware casserole (a *greixonera*), and put in the beans and the *jamón serrano* together with the herbs. After simmering for 5 minutes, add the *butifarrones* and the *sobrasada*. Continue simmering until the beans are soft; then check the seasoning; as the ham is salty, salt is not usually necessary, although a little black pepper can be added.

The dish reheats well and can be made in advance. Serve it as a side dish or starter.

MONJETES TENDRES AMB CEBA I TOMATIGA

Judias tiernas con   Green beans with
cebolla y tomate   onion and tomato

1 kg (2 ¼ lb) green beans
100 ml (3 ½ fl oz) olive
  oil
2 medium onions, minced
3 cloves of garlic, chopped

500 g (1lb) ripe tomatoes,
  skinned and chopped
50 g (2 oz) *jamón serrano,*
  diced small
salt and pepper

Top and tail the beans and, if they are large, snap them in half. Wash them well and cook them in salted boiling water until tender. Drain and leave to cool.

Now heat the oil in a large frying-pan, fry the onions until soft, then add the garlic and the tomatoes, and cook until the mixture has reduced and thickened. At this point, add the beans and ham, heat through, season and serve.

FAVES TENDRES ESTOFADES A LA MALLORQUINA

Habas tiernas estofadas
a la mallorquina

Majorcan
bean stew

This spring or autumn dish from one of Inca's famous cellar restaurants, Celler Ca'n Amer, was presented at the *II Mostra de Cuina Mallorquina* (2nd Exhibition of Majorcan Cookery) held in Palma de Mallorca in 1986. The recipe makes enough for 6 people.

200 ml (7 fl oz) olive oil
300 g (10 oz) pork loin, diced
200 g (7 oz) *tocino* or bacon, diced
170 g (6 oz) *jamón serrano*, diced
1 ¼ kg (2 ¾ lb) broad beans
a small bunch of fresh oregano and mint
2 or 3 bay leaves

250 g (9 oz) *longaniza* or *sobrasada*
4 *butifarrones*
1 bunch large spring onions, chopped including the green parts
¼ litre (9 fl oz) meat stock
1 lettuce heart, finely shredded
1 tsp mild paprika
salt and pepper

Heat the olive oil in a casserole and lightly brown all the diced meats in it. Add the shelled broad beans, cover and sweat for about 10 minutes over a very low heat. Next, add the herbs, the *sobrasada* and *butifarrones* (both whole), the spring onions and the meat stock. Cover and simmer gently until the beans are tender. Stir in the lettuce and the paprika, with salt and pepper to taste, and cook for 5 more minutes.

Now remove the *sobrasada* and *butifarrones,* cut them into thin slices, and then return them to the casserole, mixing them in well. Remove the herbs, and serve hot.

Other Vegetable Dishes

Farming has become less attractive to Majorcans with the prospect of better paid work in the tourist industry or related businesses. So fewer people now want to work on the land and many smallholdings have become fallow, often only used by their Majorcan owners as weekend retreats. Foreigners are buying up many small farmhouses and cottages as holiday or retirement homes. They arrange for local co-operatives to harvest the almonds and olives but have no need, or inclination, to grow the traditional three annual crops between the trees (one cereal crop above the soil and two root crops below). One feels that the traditional Majorcan way of life is dying out.

Once, the island was agriculturally self-supporting but now much is imported from the Spanish mainland. However, Majorcan produce is highly prized, although it often costs more. The explanation is that most of Majorca's vegetables are organically grown and require intensive labour. Divisions of land into small areas and the geography itself frequently make modern farming methods impossible. Many farmers still collect seaweed from the coast to make their own compost and follow old crop rotation systems to preserve the soil. This is a far cry from the modern farming methods which have revolutionised Andalucia, where a tractor depositing artificial fertiliser pellets can do in hours what a Majorcan farmer does in days. Stories of the Majorcan farmer who was persuaded to buy a tractor to relieve his workload abound. He gave it up after a few weeks because his work was done in a couple of hours and he had nothing to do for the rest of the day.

It is Spanish law that all vegetables on sale should be labelled with their region of origin so there should be no difficulty ascertaining whether the produce is locally grown or not.

One type of restaurant that has never had any success in Majorca is the vegetarian restaurant. Until the onset of tourism, there was widespread poverty which meant that dried pulses, vegetables, rice and bread were the staple filling foods. Wealth has converted the Majorcans into great meat eaters and vegetables have taken a secondary place. What Majorcans do nowadays is to use vegetables as ingredients in soups or casserole meat dishes, or as receptacles for stuffing, rather than as foods in their own right. But I have collected a number of recipes in which they remain the principal ingredient.

GREIXONERA D'OUS

Cazuela de huevos   Vegetable casserole with eggs

2 tbsp olive oil
1 large onion, finely
  chopped
1 large ripe tomato,
  weighing about 200 g
  (7 oz), peeled and
  chopped
2 medium potatoes, peeled
  and diced
150 g (5 oz) young broad
  beans in the pod

2 young small artichokes,
  cut into quarters
250 g (9 oz) shelled peas
1 whole head garlic
good meat stock, as needed
½ tsp of *todas especias*
  (p 47)
1 tsp dried marjoram
salt
4 hard boiled eggs

This is a dish of spring vegetables.

Heat the oil in an earthenware casserole and soften the onion in it. Add the tomato and, when it has reduced almost to a purée, add the potatoes, the broad beans still in their pods but divided into two or three, the artichokes, the peas and the whole head of garlic. Simmer for a few minutes in the tomato mixture and then pour over enough boiling meat stock to cover the vegetables. Add the spices, marjoram and salt and cook for 20 minutes.

Shell the eggs and cut them in two. Arrange on top of the casserole and let them heat through. The head of garlic can be removed before serving.

PURÉ DE PATATA A LA MALLORQUINA

Puré de patata a la   Majorcan style
mallorquina   potato purée

Make a smooth creamy purée of potatoes. Spread half of it in the bottom of a greased earthenware dish and top with thin slices of *sobrasada*. Cover with the remaining potato and sprinkle over it a mixture of grated Mahon cheese (see p 77), a little cinnamon and some toasted and pounded almonds. Dot with butter and brown in a hot oven.

PASTANAGUES MORADAS OFEGADES

Zanahorias moradas 'ofegades'   Black carrot hotpot

Purple rather than black, these carrots are a popular Majorcan vegetable, available from December to March.

12 medium black carrots	½ tsp *todas especias*
6 large spring onions,	(p 47)
finely chopped, including	salt
the green parts	½ tbsp lard, cut up
200 g (7 oz) ripe tomatoes,	1 tbsp olive oil
peeled and chopped	25 g (1 oz) *sobrasada*
25 g (1 oz) currants	1 *butifarron*
25 g (1 oz) pine nuts	2 cloves garlic, chopped

Peel the carrots and cut them into rounds. Place them in a casserole with a lid, together with the spring onions, tomatoes, currants, pine nuts, spices and a pinch of salt. Place the lard on top with the oil. Add the *sobrasada* and *butifarron,* cut into pieces, and the garlic. Place the casserole over a very low flame and heat through until the lard has melted. Cover and cook gently, shaking the casserole now and then to move the ingredients around.

After about half an hour, the carrots should be soft and the dish can be served at once. It makes a good first course. (It also reheats well and can be made in advance.)

FRIT DE VERDURES

Pisto al estilo balear Vegetables stewed in oil,
Balearic style

3 large aubergines
4 medium sized baby
marrows
2 large onions, sliced thinly
3 large green or red
peppers, seeded and cut
into large pieces

5 tbsp olive oil
5 ripe large tomatoes,
skinned and chopped
2 cloves of garlic,
roughly chopped
salt

Slice the aubergines and baby marrow into thickish rounds and cut these into cubes. All the pieces go into a colander; sprinkle with salt and cover them with a weighted plate so that the bitter juices in both vegetables are pressed out. Leave for at least half an hour. Then wash the two vegetables well in cold running water and squeeze them free of excess moisture.

Heat the olive oil in a wide, heavy-bottomed saucepan and gently fry the onions until soft but not coloured. Add the aubergines and baby marrow. After 10 minutes, add the peppers and cook for another 10 minutes. Finally, add the tomatoes and garlic and season with salt. Cover the pan and simmer gently for 30 minutes. Remove the lid and simmer for another 10 minutes. Eat hot or cold. This dish can be prepared in advance and reheated. It serves about 8 people as a side dish.

TUMBET

Cazuela de berenjenas Vegetables stewed in olive oil

Tumbet is very similar to the Provencal dish *ratatouille,* the only difference being the inclusion of potatoes in the Majorcan version. According to Luis Ripoll in *Cocina de las Baleares, tumbet* once contained bread, but this is no longer the custom. It is a versatile dish, a favourite in local restaurants where it can be served as a starter, as an accompaniment to meat or fish, or as a main dish with slices of pork loin cooked with it. A true *tumbet,* and this is why it is a summer dish only, should be made with Majorcan aubergines. These have a better flavour than other Spanish varieties and are only in season in the summer. They are cooked with other Majorcan produce: potatoes, for which the island is famous, yellowy-green peppers, tomatoes and olive oil.

½ kg (1 lb) aubergines
½ kg (1 lb) potatoes
½ kg (1 lb) green or red
   peppers
¼ litre (9 fl oz) olive oil

1 kg (2 lb) ripe tomatoes,
   skinned and chopped
4 garlic cloves, roughly
   chopped
salt

Slice the aubergines into rounds, place them in a colander and sprinkle with salt; then weigh them down with a plate for half an hour. Rinse them in cold running water and dry them. Peel the potatoes and cut them into slices. Core and de-seed the peppers and chop them into pieces.

Heat the oil. Separately fry the potatoes, peppers and aubergines, removing each from the frying pan with a slotted spoon and arranging them in layers in a casserole. Sprinkle a little salt onto each layer.

Fry the garlic in the remaining oil until just golden. Add the tomatoes and cook on a fairly high flame, stirring with a wooden spoon until it has formed a purée. Season with salt, pass through a vegetable mill or sieve and pour over the vegetables in the casserole. Cover and bake in the oven (190°C/370°F/gas mark 5) for half an hour. This dish can be served hot, warm or cold.

If you wish to make a *tumbet* with meat, fry 4 large slices of pork loin (*lomo de cerdo*) on both sides and place these between the aubergines and peppers.

See also page 109 for baked oberginos and peppers

ESPINACS AMB ALLS

Espinacas con ajos   Spinach with garlic

1 kg (2 ¼ lb) spinach	salt
2 tbsp olive oil	½ kg (1 lb) potatoes,
2 cloves of garlic, chopped	boiled with a bay leaf
1 tbsp mayonnaise, flavoured	and then mashed
with lemon juice	

Wash the spinach well and cut it up roughly. Cook it in a little boiling salted water, drain and chop finely. Heat the oil in a frying-pan and fry the garlic, adding the spinach before the garlic takes colour. Mix well, season and transfer to a warm serving plate.

Mix the mayonnaise with the hot mashed potato and arrange on the other side of the serving dish and serve with plainly cooked meat or fish.

BLEDES AMB PANSES I PINYONS

Acelgas con pasas   Swiss chard with raisins and
y piñones   pine nuts

1 ½ kg (3 ½ lb) Swiss	150 ml (5 ½ fl oz) olive
chard	oil
600 g (1 ½ lb) ripe tomatoes,	50 g (2 oz) raisins
skinned and chopped	50 g (2 oz) pine nuts
1 large onion, chopped finely	salt
2 cloves garlic, chopped	pepper

Put the raisins to soak in water for 4 hours. Wash the Swiss chard and then remove the hard stems, cook in salted water until done, and drain. When it is cool enough to handle, chop it roughly.

Now fry the onion in the oil until soft, add the tomatoes and the garlic. Cook for 10 minutes, when the sauce should have thickened, and then add the Swiss chard, the drained raisins and the pine nuts. Heat through for a further 5 minutes and serve with snippets of fried bread. This dish serves 4-6 people and is good with plainly cooked fish.

ALBORONIA

Alboronia   Aubergine and apple casserole

4 aubergines   1 large apple, peeled and
225 ml (8 fl oz) olive oil   sliced
3 fresh garlic plants (or   1 kg (2 lb) ripe tomatoes
   spring onions), roughly   ½ tbsp mild paprika
   chopped   (*pimenton rijo*)
                                     salt and pepper

Cut the aubergines into dice and sprinkle with plenty of salt.
Leave them to drain in a colander weighted down with a plate
for half to one hour. Rinse well and squeeze dry. Heat the oil and
fry the aubergines for a few minutes with the garlic plant (or
spring onion) and the apple. Place this in a casserole. Now peel
and chop the tomatoes and fry in the remaining oil until puréed.
Stir in the paprika and pour this sauce over the apples and
aubergines in the casserole. Check the seasoning and simmer,
covered, for 20 minutes. Serve hot.

ALBERGÍNIES I PEBRES AL FORN

Berenjenas y pimientos   Baked aubergines
asados   and peppers

Wash as many large, well-shaped green and red peppers and
aubergines as you need and place them in a roasting pan lightly
greased with oil. Bake in a hot oven (220°C/430°F/gas mark 7)
for 20-30 minutes, turning at least once, until the peppers are
slightly black and blistered and the aubergines soft and brown
coloured. Plunge into cold water and carefully peel off the thin
papery skin of the peppers and the tougher skin of the
aubergines.

Cut the peppers into thin strips and quarter the aubergines
lengthways, sprinkle them with salt and dress them with olive oil
and a little wine vinegar. Serve lukewarm or cold as an
accompaniment to fish or meat.

See also page 107 for tumbet.

109

GRANADA DE ALBERGÍNIES

Granada de berenjenas	Baked aubergine mould
2 kg (4½ lb) aubergines	1 kg (2 lb) ripe tomatoes,
3 large red peppers	skinned and chopped
4 cloves of garlic, finely	100 ml (3½ fl oz) dry
chopped	white wine
1 tbsp chopped parsley	1-2 tbsp finely diced
1 tsp dried marjoram	*jamón serrano*
5 eggs, beaten	a few *setas* or cultivated
for the sauce	mushrooms
2 large onions, finely	salt and pepper
chopped	2 tbsp olive oil

Peel the aubergines and cut them into finger-sized strips. Place these in a colander, sprinkle with salt and leave them covered with a weighted plate for at least half an hour. Then rinse them under cold running water, squeeze them dry, and fry them in olive oil until soft.

Bake the peppers in a hot oven until slightly black and blistered. Plunge them into cold water, peel off the papery outer skin, and remove their central cores and seeds. Cut one pepper into thin strips and reserve it. Finely chop the flesh of the other two, and mix them with the fried aubergines. Add the garlic, parsley and marjoram, and seasoning. Stir in the beaten eggs.

Grease a shallow dish or cake tin and pour in the mixture. Bake at 190°C (370°F/gas mark 4) for 25-30 minutes. The aubergine strips will now be set and coming away from the sides of the dish. Cool slightly, turn out onto a serving dish and decorate with the remaining red pepper strips.

The sauce is made thus. Fry the onions in the olive oil until almost golden. Add the tomatoes and wine. Simmer for 20-25 minutes, adding a little water if the sauce seems too thick. Pass through a sieve or vegetable mill. Return the sauce to the cleaned saucepan and add the *jamón serrano* and the mushrooms. Simmer for 5 minutes and then pour the sauce around the aubergine mould in the serving dish.

A traditional garnish for the sauce is a French omelette, allowed to cool slightly, and then cut into thin slices.

Serve this dish hot with fried potatoes.

ALBERGÍNIES FARCIDES AMB CARN

Berenjenas rellenas
con carne

Aubergines stuffed
with meat

4 large aubergines
4 tbsp olive oil
1 small onion, finely
  chopped
2 cloves of garlic, finely
  chopped
100 g (3 ½ oz) minced beef
1 large ripe tomato, of
  about 200 g (7 oz)
  peeled and chopped

1 egg
salt and pepper
for the sauce
olive oil
1 medium onion, chopped
500 g (1 lb) tomatoes,
  skinned and chopped
1 bay leaf
salt and pepper

Halve the aubergines lengthways and soak them in salted water for half an hour. Squeeze dry and scoop out the flesh, without piercing the skin. Chop the flesh finely.

Heat the olive oil in a frying-pan and fry the aubergine shells on both sides briefly, then remove and reserve.

Soften the onion in the same oil and add the garlic and mincemeat. Brown the meat, add the chopped aubergine flesh, and cook until soft. Now add the tomato and simmer gently for 10 minutes. Remove from the heat and stir in the beaten egg with plenty of seasoning. Stuff the aubergine shells with this mixture and place them in a flat baking dish.

To make the sauce: soften the onion in plenty of olive oil. Add the tomatoes and bay leaf, cook gently for 15 minutes and then add ¼ litre (9 fl oz) of water. Simmer for a further 5 minutes. Pass through a vegetable mill or sieve, season it well and pour it over the stuffed aubergine. Bake in a pre-heated oven at 190°C (370° F/gas mark 5) for 40 minutes. Serve hot.

In our oven 1 hour, and 10 minutes under the grill

ALBERGÍNIES FARCIDES

Berenjenas rellenas   Stuffed aubergines

2 large aubergines
1 large onion, very finely
  chopped
3 cloves of garlic, minced
1 tbsp fresh breadcrumbs

½ tsp oregano
a pinch of dried mint
1 egg
extra breadcrumbs
olive oil

Halve the aubergines, slash the flesh two or three times with a knife and sprinkle with salt. Place in a colander covered with a weighted plate and leave for one hour. Rinse well and squeeze dry.

Heat a little oil and fry the aubergines on both sides until soft. Take them out and leave to cool. In the same oil, fry the onion and garlic. Scoop out the flesh of the aubergines, taking care not to pierce the skins, and chop it finely. Add it to the onion mixture as well as the oregano and mint. Cook for a few minutes, then stir in the breadcrumbs. Remove from the heat, season and stir in the beaten egg. Fill the aubergine shells with this stuffing and cover with the extra breadcrumbs. Sprinkle liberally with olive oil and place in a well-oiled baking dish. Bake at 190°C (370°F, gas mark 4) for 30 minutes. Serve hot.

CALABASSONS FARCITS DE CARN

Calabacines rellenos   Baby marrows stuffed
de carne   with meat

6 baby marrows (see p 113)
100 g (3 oz) minced meat,
  either pork or beef
1 tbsp finely chopped ham
  or bacon
2 tbsp olive oil
1 small onion, chopped
2 cloves garlic, chopped

some chopped parsley
1 large ripe tomato,
  skinned and chopped
1 egg
salt and pepper
tomato sauce (see p 111,
  recipe for aubergines
  stuffed with meat)

112

Calabacin can also mean the dark green courgette, not common in Majorca. For these recipes, you need to look for the larger, pale green to whiteish-yellow baby marrows.

Plunge the baby marrows into boiling water and boil for 10 minutes. Drain them and leave to cool, then halve them lengthways and scoop out the seeds.

Fry the onion in the olive oil until soft and add the garlic, minced meat and chopped ham or bacon. Brown well, add the tomato and parsley, and cook for 10 minutes. Remove from the heat, stir in the beaten egg and season well.

Stuff the marrow halves with the meat mixture and place them in an earthenware baking dish. Pour on the tomato sauce and bake in a pre-heated oven, 190°C (370°F / gas mark 5) for 30-40 minutes.

Serve hot as a starter for 6 or a main course for 3. Or have it cold, with a salad of cooked green beans, potato, quartered hard boiled eggs and sliced tomatoes, all dressed in a little wine vinegar and plenty of virgin olive oil.

CALABASSONS FARCITS DE VERDURA

Calabacines rellenos
de verduras

Baby marrows stuffed
with vegetables

4 baby marrows
2 bunches Swiss chard
  (about 10 leaves)
salt and pepper

50 g (2 oz) grated cheese
1 egg
tomato sauce from the
  recipe on p 111

Prepare the baby marrows as in the previous recipe.

Wash the chard (removing the tough stems), and place it in a large saucepan with a little water. Bring to the boil, cover, simmer until cooked, then drain. When the chard is cool enough to handle, chop it finely and season it. Now mix in the grated cheese and the beaten egg and stuff the marrows with this mixture. Place them in an ovenproof dish and pour over the tomato sauce. Bake in a pre-heated oven at 190°C (370°F/gas mark 5) for 30 minutes.

Serve hot as a first course.

CARXOFES FARCIDES

Alcachofas rellenas   Stuffed artichokes

You can find globe or leaf artichokes in the markets for most of the year, except the summer. As a result, they are used a lot in local cooking. Small artichokes go into casserole dishes. Large ones are ideal for stuffing, and winter menus are not complete without stuffed artichokes. They can be either a fiirst or second course.

8 large artichokes	*for the sauce*
400 g (14 oz) minced beef	3 tbsp olive oil
1 small onion, finely	1 small onion, finely
chopped	chopped
2 large garlic cloves, finely	250 g (9 oz) ripe tomatoes
chopped	1 tbsp chopped parsley
1 tsp dried marjoram	1 tbsp chopped almonds
30 g (1 oz) chopped almonds	½ litre (18 fl oz) good
1 egg, beaten	meat stock
salt and pepper	

Cut off the stems of the artichokes and remove the tough outer leaves, exposing the pale green inner ones. Slice through each artichoke about 5 cm (2″) from the base. Drop each, as soon as it is prepared, into cold water mixed with lemon juice, to prevent discoloration. Cook them in boiling, salted water for 10 minutes. Remove them and rinse under cold running water. When cool enough to handle, scoop out the hairy inner chokes with a teaspoon.

Mix together the minced meat, onion, garlic, marjoram and almonds. Stir in the egg and season well. Stuff the artichokes, pushing the meat into the cavity left by the removal of the chokes and mounding it slightly.

Make the sauce by heating the oil in an ovenproof dish and frying the chopped onion until soft. Add the peeled and chopped tomatoes, the parsley and the almonds. Season well and simmer until a thick sauce has formed, then pour in the meat stock. Add the stuffed artichokes and bake, uncovered, at 180°C (355°F/ gas mark 4) for 40 minutes.

ENCIAM

Ensalata   Salad

Combine lettuce, endive, chicory, sprigs of purslane (which grows wild near cultivated ground in summer) and chopped green tomatoes; garnish with well-washed nasturtium flowers (from the garden, if you are lucky) and sliced or chopped beetroot.

In spring, young dandelion leaves are always on sale at the Olivar market in Palma. Known by their Majorcan name, *cames rotges* (red legs), they make an excellent addition to this salad. Of course, you can find your own tender dandelion leaves anywhere in the Majorcan countryside for nothing; but remember that in late spring and summer the older leaves are too tough and bitter to be used.

A good and simple dressing can be made by mixing 2 tablespoons of olive oil and ½ tablespoon wine vinegar with plenty of salt, pepper, and a little mustard.

ENCIAM AMB TREMPO

Ensalata de verano   Summer salad

Inca biscuits are small, thick, circular, hard biscuits and are sold in all grocer's shops and bakeries.

2 green peppers, diced
3 hard tomatoes, diced
1 apple, peeled and diced
1 pear, peeled and diced
2 small onions, minced
small sprigs of purslane,
   very finely chopped

4 Inca biscuits, broken
   into pieces
50 g (2 oz) capers
2 tbsp olive oil
a little wine vinegar
salt

Mix all the above salad ingredients together with the Inca biscuits in a salad bowl and dress them with the olive oil, vinegar and salt.

POMES FARCIDES

Manzanas rellenas   Stuffed apples

I remember enjoying these stuffed apples as starters in a
Majorcan restaurant, but I understand that they can also be
served as a dessert, sprinkled with sugar.

There is a small apple-growing area in the Orient valley, and
Majorcans are partial to this dish. I know that apples are not
vegetables but wanted to include this recipe and it didn't seem
to fit anywhere else.

6 large, firm dessert apples	2 tbsp boiled rice
2 onions	1 large, ripe tomato,
4 tbsp olive oil	skinned and chopped
200 g (7 oz) sausage meat	¼ litre (9 fl oz) meat
1 tbsp chopped parsley	stock
salt and pepper	

Grate one of the onions and fry in half the olive oil. When it starts
to take colour, add the sausage meat, parsley and seasoning. Fry
for 8-10 minutes. Remove from the heat and mix with the boiled
rice. This makes enough stuffing for 6 dessert apples.

Wash and core the apples and stuff them with the meat
mixture. Slit the skins around the middle and place them in a
saucepan.

Heat the rest of the oil; grate or finely chop the other onion and
fry until soft. Add the tomato and simmer until a thick sauce has
formed. Add the stock, bring to the boil, then pour over the
apples. Cover and simmer for 20-30 minutes. If you would like
the sauce thicker, just add a grated apple 10 minutes before the
end of cooking time.

Fish

With a fishing fleet reputed to be as large as those of all the other EEC nations put together, Spaniards obviously eat a lot of fish; indeed they eat, per head of the population, about eight times more than the British.

So seafood is a very important element in Spanish cookery; and Majorca is no exception as far as local knowledge of and dedication to the cooking of fish is concerned.

But over 80% of the Balearic fishing fleet is made up of small, often family-owned boats, known locally as *llauts*. Due to their small size, they can only fish in coastal waters. This brings an immediacy to the local fishing industry, for, by dint of working close to home, these coastal fishermen can supply the freshest fish. I have frequently walked around Palma's Santa Catalina market and seen fish on sale that were still (just) alive. In fact all the Majorcan markets, when presenting their varied selection of fresh fish, can offer something that is only a few hours out of the sea. In face of this bounty, I feel that it would be sacrilege to choose frozen fish.

Although fresh fish is readily available throughout Majorca, the two main Palma markets, the Olivar and Santa Catalina, offer the widest choice. The enormous Olivar market, situated on two floors in the centre of Palma, caters for hotels and restaurants as well as for the domestic shopper. This means that it is terribly busy, but is worth the battle because it is the best place to buy live lobster and crabs, prawns and a great variety of other shellfish as well as a wide range of local fish. The smaller Santa Catalina market also offers an excellent variety, but its turnover is fast — by midday there is usually little choice left in the fish section whereas in the Olivar market there will still be a reasonable selection. (Both markets usually close at 2 pm.)

Much of Majorcan fish cookery is simplicity itself, for there is really no better way to emphasize the natural flavour than by the

117

plainest cooking; and, as Majorca does not produce dairy goods, there is no tradition of rich cream sauces. The fish can be either grilled (*a la parilla*), cooked on a hot plate (*a la plancha*) or dipped in flour and fried in olive oil (*frito*). It may be accompanied by a slice of lemon or by a simple sauce based on the local produce: tomatoes, olive oil, garlic, almonds, pine nuts and capers (although mayonnaise or *aioli,* nearly always homemade, is the common restaurant accompaniment).

As great fish eaters, Majorcans regard the head as almost the best part of the fish, so there are many recipes for cooking fish whole — and most fish are best cooked whole. Many of the recipes are for baked fish. By combining local produce, especially seasonal vegetables, with fish, distinctive dishes are produced.

I am sure that I am not alone in disliking fish which have a lot of small bones. It is worth remembering that sharks (a class which includes dogfish) and rays, being primitive forms of fish, have no true bones, just cartilaginous skeletons which cause the diner no problem at all. Of the other fish, the larger ones, naturally, have larger bones, which can easily be avoided. And tiny fish have bones which are so small that they can just be eaten. The problem arises over smallish fish like the red mullet, the smaller of the sea breams, and large sardines. These do have troublesome bones — too big to be eaten, too small to be easily extricated. Here I can only say that it is possible to learn how to take them apart (not that I'm much good at it myself) and that the flavour of fresh red mullet in particular makes the effort well worthwhile.

SARDINES

Sardinas   Sardines

For catching sardines, *llauts* or similar small boats are rigged up with a cluster of three or four propane lamps suspended over the stern and as evening falls are towed out to sea in groups by larger fishing boats. Once the lamps are lit, a brilliant pool of light attracts large shoals of sardines and the accompanying boat proceeds to encircle them in nets. I remember once, when out fishing for squid by the light of just one propane lamp, we attracted a shoal of tiny sardines who just swarmed around the light. All I had to do was lean over the side and scoop up as many as I liked in a hand net. The obvious ease with which sardines are caught is reflected in their price — they are amongst the most inexpensive fish in the Mediterranean.

The tiny sardines which appear frequently throughout the year in the fish markets and shops can be deep fried like whitebait, but make a much tastier dish — 250 g (9 oz) is sufficient for four people as an appetizer.

Never fry a large batch all at once, for they will stick together in a big lump. Simply dust the sardines with seasoned flour and deep fry them a few at a time in hot olive oil, to obtain the best possible flavour and crispness. Serve at once, to preserve the crispness, with nothing more than lemon wedges.

Small fresh anchovies (*boquerones*) can be treated in the same manner. They have a lighter taste than the sardines.

Larger sardines, cleaned, scaled, dipped in flour and fried in olive oil are a classic dish throughout Spain, and four per person make an excellent first course. But nowadays filleted sardines are becoming very popular in Majorca. Dipped in flour, fried in olive oil and served with lemon, or baked in an earthenware dish with tomato sauce, they are almost a convenience food.

ALATXAS AMB SALSA DE TOMATIGUES
I PEBRES

Alachas con salsa de   Sardines with tomato
tomate y pimientos   and pepper sauce

There seems to be an affinity between certain fish and tomatoes
and peppers which Majorcan cookery explores to the full; yet the
resulting dishes never appear to be the same. *Alacha* is *Sardinella
aurita,* one of the larger species of sardine. Although *alachas* are
sometimes sold filleted it is a simple task to do at home — slit the
fish on the underside from head to tail and remove the head, guts
and backbone but leave the tail intact. Open the fish out flat and
rinse under running water, easing off the scales as you do so. Lay
on a plate and sprinkle with salt and lemon juice and marinate
for one hour. One kilo (2 lb) of *alachas* will serve four people as
a main course.

First, make a tomato sauce by finely chopping one onion and
softening it in a frying-pan with a little olive oil. Add 1 kg (2 lb)
of very ripe tomatoes, skinned and finely chopped, and cook
gently until a thick sauce has formed. Cut two large green
peppers into 4 cm (1½") squares and add them to the sauce
together with as many whole unpeeled garlic cloves as you like.
Season with salt and pepper and simmer until the pepper is soft.

Meanwhile, coat the fish in flour and fry in hot olive oil on
both sides until golden brown. Place them in an earthenware
serving dish, pour the sauce over them, and pop the dish into a
hot oven (200°C/400°F/gas mark 6) for 10 minutes. Serve at
once with fresh bread, and a salad to follow.

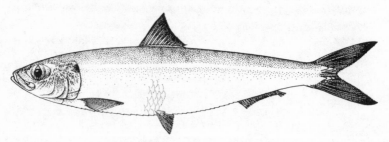

Sardinella aurita, *known as* alacha

RAORS

Raones   Cleaver wrasse

Raors, small fish whose scientific name is *Xyrichthys novacula,* are rare and very expensive. They are available spasmodically in Palma's Olivar Market, from the end of August to the middle of October, when they make a brief appearance in Majorca's coastal waters. I have heard it said that *raors* appear only off the Majorcan coast and off the coast of Japan, but I have never been able to verify this story; and now I hear that they are also known on parts of the French and Italian coasts. Fished for with great enthusiasm during their short season — by professionals for the large sums of money which they fetch and by amateurs for the delicate fish itself — they provide a pleasant morning's activity using line and bait in inshore waters.

Raors are thin-bodied and quite pretty, of a salmony pink to orange colour. They must first be scaled. Some cooks gut them; others do not. Either way, the fish is salted and dipped in flour. It is then quickly fried in olive oil, which should not be too hot, until golden on both sides — it takes just a few minutes.

These fish are not at all fiddly to eat having a delicate white flesh that comes away easily from the spine.

Xyrichthys novacula, *known as* roar in *Majorca*

MOLLS A LES GRAELIES

Salmonetes a la parilla   Grilled red mullet

Red mullet are highly prized throughout the Mediterranean, where they are available all year round. They are ideal fish for a summer barbecue, preferably a charcoal one, as in this recipe. But it requires some skill to avoid the tiny bones when eating them.

4 large or 8 small red mullet
salt and pepper
juice of 2 lemons
70 ml (2½ fl oz) olive oil

1 tbsp finely chopped parsley
2 cloves garlic, peeled and chopped

When red mullets are to be grilled or fried, it is not normal to gut them, though most restaurants in Majorca will do so unless asked not to — it is a matter of choice. Do not remove the scales. Put the fish into a container and sprinkle with salt, pepper, the juice of one lemon and the olive oil. Leave to marinate for one hour.

Grill the fish over a hot charcoal barbecue, brushing them regularly with the marinade. Four minutes on each side will be sufficient if they are large ones. When cooked remove the scales — they will have coalesced into a thick 'skin' that is easy to take off with a fork.

Place the fish on a serving dish and sprinkle with the parsley mixed with the garlic, and the remaining lemon juice, and serve at once.

MOLLS AL FORN

Salmonetes al horno   Baked red mullet

4 large red mullet   100 g (3 ½ oz) fresh
juice of one lemon   breadcrumbs
1 tbsp olive oil   15 g (½ oz) butter
3 tbsp heated fish stock   salt

Scale the fish by rubbing a knife along them from tail to head, or use a special implement rather like a potato peeler with a serrated edge. Clean them but leave them whole.

Season the fish with salt and arrange them in an ovenproof dish. Sprinkle them with lemon juice and pour over the olive oil and the hot fish stock. Cover with the breadcrumbs and place a nut of butter on top of each fish. Bake in a moderate oven (180°C/335°F/gas mark 4) for half an hour, and bring the dish straight from the oven to the table.

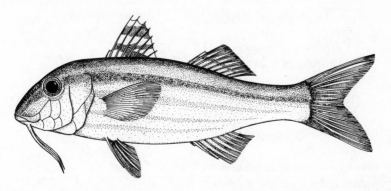

Mullus surmuletus, *one of the red mullets*

SERVIOLA AMB SALSA MALLORQUINA

Pez de limon con salsa   Amberjack with a
mallorquina   Majorcan sauce

The amberjack (*serviola*) is a sizeable and handsome fish which is found in one form or another in most warm waters round the world. The reputation of these fish varies considerably, but they are highly esteemed by the Majorcans. Generally available all year round, they are particularly plentiful through the summer, autumn and early winter months. Specimens weighing 3-4 kg (7-9 lb) or more are generally sold cut into steaks while those around the 1-1½ kg (2-3 lb) mark are good for baking whole.

1 whole amberjack weighing about 1½ kg (3 lb plus)
1 large onion, finely sliced
½ a big carrot stuck with 6 or 7 cloves
½ litre (18 fl oz) red wine
250 ml (9 fl oz) olive oil
2 large leeks, finely sliced
2 large spring onions
250 g (½ lb) ripe tomatoes
3 cloves of garlic, chopped
1 tbsp finely chopped parsley
1 tsp mild paprika
salt
freshly ground black pepper
100 g (3½ oz) pine nuts
100 g (3½ oz) raisins
4 large potatoes

Place the sliced onion in a saucepan with the clove-studded carrot and the red wine. Boil briskly until reduced by one third.

In a large frying-pan heat a little of the oil and gently fry the leeks and spring onions until soft. Add the tomatoes and the chopped garlic and continue to cook gently until a thick sauce has formed; then remove from the heat. Now stir in the parsley, the paprika and the seasoning, followed by the onion-and-wine mixture (after removing the carrot), the pine nuts and the raisins.

Peel and thinly slice the potatoes. Grease an ovenproof baking dish large enough to hold the fish and lay the sliced potatoes on the bottom.

Scale and gut the amberjack, then score it diagonally on both sides two or three times. Lay it on top of the potatoes and season well. Cover it completely with the onion mixture, which will be a lovely cinnamon colour, pour the remaining olive oil over all and bake in a moderate oven (180°C/355°F/gas mark 4) for one hour.

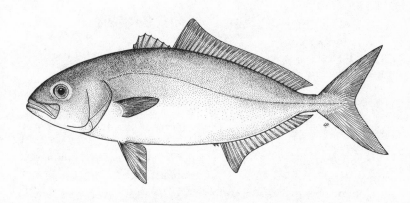

above, the amberjack, Seriola dumerili: *below, the most common of the Mediterranean groupers,* Epinephelus guaza

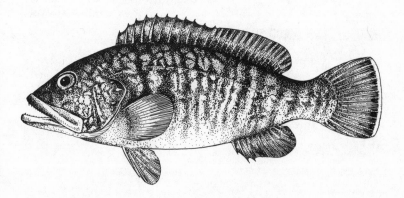

SERVIOLA O ANFOS A LA MALLORQUINA

Pez de limon o mero   Amberjack or grouper
a la mallorquina   Majorcan style

A simpler version of the preceding recipe, with the fish cut into
steaks, which makes for easier serving. This is very similar to the
various *a la mallorquina* fish dishes of Majorcan restaurants.
Grouper, a firm-fleshed fish with a delicate flavour, is a fine
alternative to amberjack.

This recipe serves 6.

1 ½ kg (3 ¼ lb) amberjack   1 bunch spinach (a large
  or grouper steaks   handful)
150 ml (5 fl oz) olive oil   50 g (2 oz) pine nuts
4 large spring onions   50 g (2 oz) raisins
200 g (7 oz) ripe tomatoes   ½ kg (1 lb) potatoes
½ kg (1 lb) green peppers   seasoned flour

Roughly slice the spring onions, including the green parts, and
gently fry them in some of the olive oil in a frying pan. When they
are soft, add the peeled and chopped tomatoes and cook gently
until almost puréed. Cut up the peppers and add these to the pan
together with the washed and shredded spinach, pine nuts and
raisins. Season with salt and pepper, cook gently over a low heat
for a minute or two, then remove from the heat.

Now peel the potatoes and slice them very thinly. Lightly
grease an ovenproof baking dish and lay the slices on the bottom.
Place the fish slices on top and season well. Cover with the
vegetable mixture and pour the olive oil over. Bake in a
moderate oven (180°C/355°F/gas mark 4) for 35-45 minutes.

ESCABETX DE PEIX

Escabeche de pescado   Marinated fried fish

In 1986 the Second Exhibition of Majorcan Cooking was held at
Palma; and this recipe, from the Restaurante Sa Sinia of Porto
Colom, was among those presented at it. It calls for the use of
a number of different fish. Choose several from: tuna, bonito,
dolphin fish, sea bream, picarel, skate.

Quantities serve 6.

1 ¼ kg (2 ¾ lb) fish (see above)	8 garlic cloves, peeled
salt and pepper	1 onion, finely sliced
flour for coating the fish	1 large carrot, finely sliced
300 ml (10 fl oz) olive oil	1 tsp mild paprika
4 thin slices lemon	200 ml (7 fl oz) wine vinegar
4 bay leaves	200 ml (7 fl oz) dry white wine
parsley sprigs	100 ml (3 ½ fl oz) water

Small fish such as picarel should simply be scaled, cleaned and
beheaded. Larger ones should be cut into steaks or pieces.

Season the fish well and coat them lightly with flour, then fry
them until golden on both sides in the olive oil. Remove them
and drain them well, then place them in a deep serving dish.
Arrange the lemon slices, bay leaves and sprigs of parsley on top.

In what is left of the olive oil fry the garlic cloves for a few
seconds, then add the onion and carrot. Leave to fry gently on
a low heat until the onion is soft. Next, stir in the paprika and
pour in the vinegar and wine. Bring to a simmer, still over a low
heat, then remove.

Leave to cool, stirring in the water to speed the process. When
the liquid is cold, pour it over the fish, making sure that it is well
covered. Store in the refrigerator, where it will keep well for up
to a week.

Serve the fish and a little of the marinade and vegetables at
room temperature, with fresh bread.

PEIX EN ES FORN

Pescado al horno   Fish baked in the oven

Don Andres Vera of Puerto de Andraitx, who in his time was both fisherman and hotelier, contributes this recipe: a more robust version of the two preceding *mallorquina* dishes.

1 kg (2¼ lb) amberjack,
  grouper or hake steaks
3 large potatoes
2 large spring onions
1 bunch (a large handful)
  of Swiss chard
200 g (7 oz) ripe tomatoes,
  peeled

½ cauliflower
¼ kg (½ lb) young broad
  beans in their pods (or
  substitute green beans)
1 tbsp chopped parsley
225 ml (8 fl oz) olive oil
salt
freshly ground black pepper

Peel the potatoes and slice them very thinly. Cover the bottom of an oiled baking dish with them, lay the fish steaks on top and season well.

  Roughly chop the spring onions (including the green parts), the chard and the tomatoes, and mix all this together with the parsley. Divide the cauliflower into florets and blanch these for one minute. Cut the broad beans in their pods into small pieces and blanch them too. Then mix the cauliflower and beans with the other vegetables and spread the whole lot over the fish. Season, pour the olive oil over all, and bake in a medium oven (180°C/355°F/gas mark 4) for about 45 minutes.

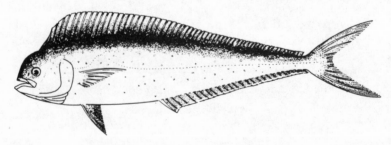

the dolphin fish, Coryphaena hippurus

LLAMPUGA AMB PEBRES

Dorado con pimientos   Dolphin fish with peppers

The dolphin fish (which has no connection with the dolphin, which is a mammal) is in the markets for just a short season, September to November. It is always called by its Majorcan name *llampuga,* very close to the name *lampuki,* by which it is very well known in Malta. It is very good to eat, and worth seeking out, but rarely seen on a restaurant menu. Here is the most popular of the various Majorcan recipes for it.

1 whole dolphin fish weighing 1½ kg (3¼ lb)	½ kg (1 lb) ripe tomatoes
salt	1 whole head of garlic
lemon juice	275 ml (10 fl oz) olive oil
1 kg (2 lb) red peppers	flour to coat the fish

Clean, wash and drain the dolphin fish. Remove the head and tail and cut the body into thick steaks. Sprinkle these with salt and squeeze lemon juice over them, then leave them to marinate for an hour.

Deseed the peppers and cut them into pieces. Skin the tomatoes. Break up the head of garlic and peel each clove, gently crushing it but keeping it whole.

Put half the olive oil in a large frying-pan and fry the peppers with the garlic until soft. In another frying-pan, heat the remaining olive oil and gently cook the tomatoes in it until they have formed a thick sauce.

Once the peppers are soft, remove them from the first pan. Coat the fish steaks in flour and fry them in the same oil (adding a little more if necessary) until they are well cooked on both sides.

Arrange the fish in a large shallow earthenware dish, cover with the peppers and garlic, and pour the tomato sauce over all. Bake in a moderately hot oven (200°C/400°F/gas mark 6) for 15 minutes.

This dish can be served hot or cold.

BULLIT DE PEIX AMB PATATES I CEBAS

Hervido de pescado con   Poached fish with
patatas y cebollas   potatoes and onions

Very fresh firm-fleshed fish such as scorpion fish (*cap roig*) and John Dory (*gallo*), are delicious cooked like this. It is a good dish to order in a restaurant.

By the way, the Mallorquin name for John Dory, *gallo*, can cause a great deal of confusion amongst non-Spaniards, for the same word in Castilian Spanish means 'cockerel'. There is a very well-known restaurant in Palma called El Gallo, which has the cockerel as its symbol and is full of cockerel paintings and statuettes. Foreigners naturally assumed when they ordered *gallo* from the menu that they would be served something like *coq au vin*. You can imagine their surprise when John Dory appeared. The dish was subsequently withdrawn.

1 kg (2 ¼ lb) John Dory or
    scorpion fish
1 litre (36 fl oz) water
2 large onions, peeled and
    quartered

2 large potatoes, peeled
    and quartered
salt
olive oil
wine vinegar

Place the onions and potatoes in a large saucepan (big enough to take the fish in one piece) containing the water, salted and already boiling. Continue to boil until the potatoes are nearly cooked.

Meanwhile scale the fish and snip off their fins, especially the spiny rays of the scorpion fish. Gut them, but leave the liver in place and keep the fish whole. Make two deep incisions in the body.

Now add the fish to the saucepan, keeping the water just on boiling point, ie bubbling gently. A John Dory will cook in about 12 minutes, while a scorpion fish will take about 15-20 minutes.

Remove the fish carefully and divide into two portions. Make sure you include the head, which in both fish contains some flesh and is considered a delicacy. Drain the potatoes and onions, and serve them with the fish, sprinkling salt, vinegar and lots of good olive oil over everything.

The broth makes good fish stock; or it can be served as the first course with thin slices of toast (rubbed with a garlic clove), and a *picada* (p 46) added.

above, the John Dory, Zeus faber: *below, the large scorpion fish,*
Scorpaena scrofa

THE SEA BREAM FAMILY

This is the largest family of Mediterranean fish, with more than 20 species. They vary in size and quality, but generally speaking they are not too big to be cooked whole and they make good, sometimes excellent, eating. Fishing for them is quite intensive, so the catch includes many young specimens, well below the maximum size. Common species are: *pargo* (sea bream — it is the archetypal species and the largest in this little list), *dorado* (gilt-head, generally reckoned to be the finest), *besugo* (red bream), *oblada* (saddled bream), and *cantera* (black bream). All the year round one is likely to find these fish in Majorcan markets, in sizes of about 20 cm (8″) in length and weighing roughly ½ kg (1 lb). These are ideal for baking whole, one per person, and the way of doing this is very simple.

Scale and gut the fish and lay them in a well-oiled baking dish. Score the upper side of each fish diagonally in two or three places and insert lemon slices into the cuts. Season the fish, pour plenty of olive oil over them, and bake them in a medium oven (180°C/355°F/gas mark 4) for 25-30 minutes. When you serve them, pour some of the pan juices over each fish and sprinkle them with a mixture of parsley and garlic, both chopped.

That attends to the youngsters. Larger fish of the same family can be cooked according to the next recipe.

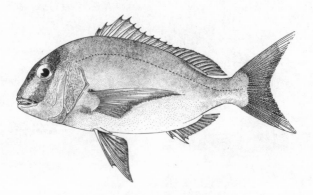

the common sea bream, Pargus pargus

CANTERA DE LES ILLES

Chopa de las islas   Black bream of the islands

Two other relatively large members of the family which suit this
recipe are *denton* (dentex) and *dorada* (gilt-head).

1 black bream weighing
  1 ¼ kg (2 ¾ lb) uncleaned
salt and pepper
2 lemons, thickly sliced
½ kg (1 lb) potatoes
1 onion
250 g (½ lb) tomatoes

2 cloves garlic
450 ml (16 fl oz) dry white
  wine
225 ml (8 fl oz) olive oil
½ tsp dried thyme
finely chopped parsley
1 bay leaf

Scale and gut the fish, wash it under running water, dry it, and
put it in an oven dish. Make several deep diagonal cuts on the
upper side, sprinkle with salt and pepper, and insert slices of
lemon into the incisions.

    Peel and thinly slice the potatoes and onion. Skin and halve
the tomatoes. Arrange all these around the fish, together with the
remaining lemon slices. Pour the wine and olive oil over all.
Season with salt and pepper, sprinkle on the thyme and parsley,
and place the bay leaf on top. Bake in a moderate oven (180°C/
355°F/gas mark 4) for between 45 minutes and one hour, until
cooked through.

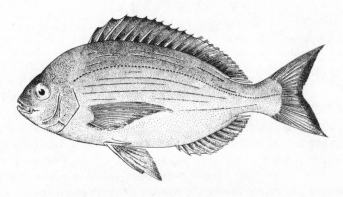

Spondyliosoma cantharus, *the black sea bream,* cantera *in Mallorquin*

133

EMPERADOR AMB PEBRES AL FORN

Pez espada con pimientos Baked swordfish
al horno with tomatoes

Swordfish, always known as *emperador* in Majorca, has somewhat
dry flesh, and I have never thought that the standard restaurant
treatment of grilling the steaks or cooking them on the *plancha*
does it justice. The following method of cooking with tomatoes
and peppers produces a more succulent dish. Swordfish steaks
are ideal for people who don't like small bones and are available
all year round.

4 swordfish steaks 1 glass dry white wine
1 bay leaf 250 ml (9 fl oz) water
1 small carrot 6 black peppercorns
½ onion salt
1 stick celery

Combine all the above ingredients, except the swordfish, and
bring to the boil. Simmer for 10 minutes and add the fish steaks.
When the liquid returns to the boil, simmer the fish for exactly
two minutes. Remove and drain, discarding the cooking liquid.

125 ml (4½ fl oz) olive oil 100g (3½ oz) black and
½ onion, finely chopped green olives, stoned
1 chopped garlic clove 2 tsp capers
400 g (14 oz) tomatoes, salt and pepper
  peeled and chopped 100 g (3½ oz) fresh
3 large green peppers breadcrumbs
2 large red or yellow
  peppers
1 tbsp finely chopped
  parsley

Heat the oil in a large saucepan and add the onion and garlic.
Fry for a few minutes until the onion is soft, then add the
chopped tomatoes, plus the peppers in pieces about 2 cm (¾")
square. Stir in the parsley and season well. Simmer for 20
minutes, stirring occasionally to prevent the sauce from sticking
to the bottom.

Oil an ovenproof dish and put in half the pepper mixture. Sprinkle on half the olives and half the capers and arrange the fish on top. Add the remaining olives and capers, and the rest of the peppers, and cover with the breadcrumbs. Drizzle olive oil over the breadcrumbs and bake for 20 minutes in a medium oven (180°C/355°F/gas mark 4).

This dish can be eaten hot or cold.

RATJADA O MUSSOLA FRITA

Raya o musola frita   Fried skate or dogfish

Skate, a staple of English fish and chips shops, is cheap all year round in Majorca. Only the 'wings' of a skate are edible and they are usually ready for cooking. These 'wings' have thick strands of cartilaginous 'bone' running through them but the flesh, after cooking, is easily removed from them.

1 kg (2 lb) of skate, cleaned weight, will be sufficient for four to five people. Have the fishmonger cut it into pieces, then wash them well in cold running water to remove any bitterness and marinate for 2 to 3 hours in a little vinegar, salt, pepper, a few sprigs of parsley, some chopped onion and a few roughly chopped garlic cloves. Drain, dry, dip each piece in seasoned flour, and fry on both sides in olive oil until golden brown.

Another fish which is always available and is good value for money is *musola,* one of the dogfish which belong to the shark family. It is sold cut into steaks which should be marinated in lemon juice and salt for an hour or so, then coated lightly in seasoned flour and fried in olive oil until golden on both sides.

Either *tumbet* (p 106) or baked aubergines and peppers (p 109) will make an excellent accompaniment to these dishes.

BACALLÁ

Bacalao   Salt cod

In the days of strict Roman Catholicism, when the church did not allow people to eat meat on fast days, salt was used to preserve the large amounts of fish consumed. Nowadays religion has little hold over domestic life, but the acquired taste for salt cod ensures that it is still eaten with regularity and, indeed, relish. It now features on many a restaurant menu.

My first experience of salt cod was very nearly my last! It was far too salty for my taste. I soon discovered that the 24-hour soaking recommended by nearly every cookery book dealing with the subject is not enough, and many of my Majorcan friends agree. I soak salt cod, with several changes of water, for 48 hours. Then I rinse it and pat it dry with kitchen paper before cutting it into manageable pieces, free of skin and bone.

Once prepared, salt cod cooks quickly, taking only 10 to 15 minutes, depending on the thickness of the pieces. Some people just soak it and then eat it uncooked. They say that this is very good, but I have never been tempted to try it. The simplest and most common way of cooking it in Majorca is to coat the fish pieces in flour seasoned only with pepper, then to fry them in olive oil until golden. Fresh tomato sauce is poured over the fried pieces.

All the weekly markets and the large permanent Palma markets have one or two stalls selling salt cod, where they will slice off the required amount with a guillotine. However, the supermarkets usually sell salt cod wrapped in plastic — this is not so good and I strongly recommend that you buy it 'loose' from the markets.

Salt cod has a very strong smell, which I dislike. Although you can keep it for months, I think that it is best, and easier on the nose, to buy according to your needs, soaking the fish as soon as you have bought it.

BORRIDA DE BACALLÁ

'Borrida' de bacalao   Salt cod with a bread and
                                                 onion sauce

As the title of the recipe suggests, this dish is related to the well
known *bourride* of the south of France.

The quantities given serve 4, as usual, but only for a first
course or a light main course.

600 g (1 ⅓ lb) salt cod,   2 slices of bread
  prepared as described   125 ml (4 ½ fl oz) milk
  on page 136   2 tsp mild paprika
1 large onion, finely   ground nutmeg to taste
  chopped   ground black pepper
125 ml (4 ½ fl oz) olive oil   to taste
2 large garlic cloves
1 tbsp chopped parsley

Heat the oil in a shallow earthenware dish (or frying-pan) and
soften the onion in this, without allowing it to take colour; then
add the prepared pieces of salt cod and fry them gently for 5
minutes.

Meanwhile soak the bread in the milk, then squeeze it dry
reserving the milk which is squeezed out. Pound the garlic and
parsley in a mortar, add the bread and the paprika, and continue
pounding until you have a paste. Add this to the salt cod together
with the reserved milk and simmer for 5 minutes, stirring often.
(If you want a thinner sauce, add a little more milk.)

Finally, sprinkle on the nutmeg and pepper and serve at once,
very hot.

GUISAT DE BACALLÁ

Guisado de bacalao   Casserole of salt cod and vegetables

600 g (1 ⅓ lb) salt cod,
  soaked in several changes
  of water for 48 hours
1 onion
2 cloves garlic
1 large ripe tomato, about
  200 g (7 oz)
3 tbsp olive oil
1 heaped tsp mild paprika
1 tbsp chopped parsley

½ litre (18 fl oz) water
100 g (3 ½ oz) shelled
  peas
250 g (9 oz) potatoes,
  peeled and cut into
  dice
200 g (7 oz) cauliflower,
  divided into small
  florets

Rinse and dry the salt cod and cut into small pieces, removing all skin and bone. Finely chop the onion and garlic and skin and chop the tomato.

Heat the oil in an earthenware casserole (a *greixonera*), and soften the onion in this. Then add the garlic and tomato, and simmer until a thick sauce has formed.

Next, stir in the paprika and parsley and pour in the water. When the liquid begins to boil, put in the peas, potatoes and cauliflower and simmer for 20 minutes. Add the salt cod and continue to simmer for 15 minutes, stirring often.

Other Seafoods

What the French call *fruits de mer* are *marisc* in Mallorquin and *mariscos* in Castilian. There is no English word which can correctly be applied to the lot of them.

Anyway, here we start with crustaceans (lobster, crab, prawn), and then go on to molluscs. The large molluscs, such as octopus, squid and cuttlefish, have no external shell and present a floppy and to some eyes repulsive appearance; but they are excellent food. Smaller molluscs, creatures such as whelks or mussels, which live in single or double shells, are what can properly be called 'shellfish', though the term is often used with a wider application. These true shellfish are represented here by just one recipe for mussels, though various clams are to be found in Majorcan markets (and can be cooked in a similar way).

The drawing below shows a spiny lobster, undoubtedly the queen of Mediterranean crustaceans.

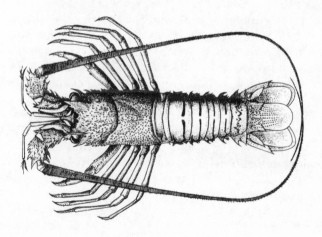

one of the Mediterranean spiny lobsters, Palinurus elephas

139

LLAGOSTA

Langosta   Spiny lobster

Fresh lobster is very expensive throughout the Mediterrenean and Majorca is no exception. Though it is only in season from the beginning of April to the end of August, the main fish markets and shops are spasmodically supplied out of season by local commercial concerns which keep live lobsters, brought during the summer, in *viveros* (fishtanks).

Although the spiny lobsters of the Mediterranean (also known as crawfish or rock lobsters) lack the formidable claws of the North Atlantic lobster, and therefore, size for size, offer less meat, they are just as good.

In a restaurant, try having *Langosta a la plancha*. The live lobster is split from head to tail by a single blow which kills it instantly and is then grilled on a hot plate, first with the shell side down to set the meat, then with the cut side down to lightly toast it. It is served hot with a dressing of olive oil or with home-made mayonnaise.

Splitting the live lobster is a messy job, so if cooking at home you would probably prefer this simpler recipe.

Buy your lobster live. Plunge it into a large saucepan of boiling, heavily salted or (better) sea water. (Most chefs I have talked to say this is more humane than putting the lobster in cold water and bringing it slowly to the boil; but some authorities concerned with animal welfare disagree.) When the water has reboiled allow 30 minutes for the first kilo and 20 minutes for each subsequent kilo. Then remove the lobster and plunge it into a bowl of cold water to prevent further cooking.

The lobster lunch I once attended, an annual event in this particular family on the last day of its fishing season, consisted of a huge tray on which had been arranged shredded lettuce, tomatoes, hard boiled eggs, potato salad and several large boiled lobsters, split open, cut into pieces, piped with home-made mayonnaise and garnished with slices of red pepper. We ended the lunch with melon from the garden. Simple but very memorable!

CALDERETA DE LLAGOSTA

Caldereta de langosta   Lobster casserole

A popular dish which originates from the neighbouring island of
Minorca, famous for its lobsters; but Majorcans have made
caldereta almost their own. This is how it is prepared at the
Restaurant Miramar in Puerto de Andraitx. Juan St Juan, the
owner, emphasizes that it is a summer dish, for live lobsters
bought out of season are just not the same. The name *caldereta*
refers to the earthenware casserole in which the lobster is cooked
and served.

2 kg (4½ lb) live lobster	2 litres (72 fl oz) water
2 onions	200 ml (7 fl oz) olive oil
500 g (1 lb 2 oz) ripe	200 g (7 oz) very thinly
tomatoes	sliced Majorcan country
1 whole head garlic	bread (*pan payes*)

Hold your lobster firmly (using a towel) by the body from above
and press it down hard. Using a sharp pointed knife, pierce the
carapace just behind the head; this is supposed to sever the spinal
cord and kill it instantly. Next, cut it in half lengthways and
remove the gut (visible as a dark line running the length of the
tail section) as well as the stomach sac in the head section. Then
cut it into small pieces. Set the water to boil in a casserole,
preferably of earthenware. Meanwhile, in a frying pan, heat up
the oil and fry the pieces of lobster until the shell turns red; then
remove and reserve them.

Add the finely chopped onion and garlic to the remaining
oil in the frying-pan and fry until the onion is soft. Now add
the peeled and chopped tomato and cook gently for 5 minutes.
Liquidize this tomato mixture in the blender, sieve it, and add
it with the lobster pieces to the boiling water in the casserole.
Bring back to the boil and leave to simmer for 20 minutes.
Finally, add salt to taste.

Serve in soup plates lined with the finely sliced bread.

CRANCS

Cangrejos   Crabs

There are more kinds of crab available in the Mediterranean than in Britain; but they are not cheap. Mediterranean recipes, as Alan Davidson points out in his *Mediterranean Seafood*, may not be as suitable for really large crabs as recipes which come from the North Atlantic area; but Mediterranean cooks have been more inventive in dealing with smaller crabs which would probably be ignored elsewhere. In my opinion, however, crab dishes are not particularly good ones to choose in Majorcan restaurants.

The spider crab (shown below) is the most available large crab, though the large-clawed edible crab of the Mediterranean (almost identical with its Atlantic brother, the one regularly sold in Britain) is becoming more common.

Buy either of these crabs alive and follow the instructions for boiling a lobster, if you wish to serve boiled crab with mayonnaise. Prise off the upper shell and remove the stomach bag and gills before serving.

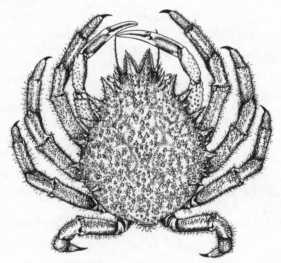

the spider crab, Maja squinado

GUISAT DE CRANCA

Guisado de centollo   Spider crab stew

In Majorcan cookery, the following recipe is more usual than boiled crab with mayonnaise. It calls for spider crab, but works just as well with the large edible crab, and provides a hearty crab stew for two people.

1 spider crab weighing about 1 kg (2 ¼ lb)	grated nutmeg
4 tbsp olive oil	ground white pepper
1 onion	salt
3 large ripe tomatoes	100 ml (3 ½ fl oz) red wine
2 garlic cloves	200 g (7 oz) potatoes, peeled weight, diced
1 tbsp chopped fresh parsley	1 bay leaf
1 tsp paprika	

Plunge the live crab into rapidly boiling water for exactly 2 minutes, then remove it directly to a bowl of cold water. When it is cool, prise off the upper shell and remove the stomach bag and the gills. Cut the body in half and crack the claws.

Heat the oil in a casserole and soften the finely chopped onion for 10 minutes before adding the peeled and chopped tomatoes, the chopped garlic and parsley and simmer gently until it has become a thick sauce. Season with the paprika, nutmeg, white pepper and salt and pour in the red wine and a little water. Bring to the boil and stir in the peeled and diced potatoes and the bay leaf. Simmer for 10 minutes, or longer if necessary. Add the pieces of crab, pour in just enough water to cover, and bring back to the boil. Then simmer gently for 20 minutes more.

Serve at once with fresh bread — and large napkins, as extracting the meat from the crab can be messy.

143

GAMBES

Gambas   Prawns

The various prawns available differ in size and to some extent in price, though their great popularity tends to make them all expensive. They are generally sold uncooked — unlike Britain where cooked prawns are the norm. Don't forget that you are dealing with fresh ones!

There are two popular ways of preparing prawns. GAMBAS HERVIDAS, boiled prawns, is the simplest. Just snap off the large whiskers and put the prawns into a pan of boiling, very salty water. By the time the water comes back to the boil very small prawns will probably be done; larger ones will need about 5 minutes boiling. Allow to cool slightly and serve just as they are with some lemon slices.

A more common restaurant dish is GAMBAS A LA PLANCHA, prawns cooked on a hot plate. Use a heavy-bottomed frying-pan if you don't have a *plancha*. Wash some large prawns, snapping off the long whiskers. Dry the prawns well, sprinkle them with salt, lemon juice and olive oil, and place them at once on a very hot *plancha*. Turn them several times while they cook; and at each turn brush them with a little more olive oil. They should be done within 15 minutes. Serve at once sprinkled with a mixture of freshly chopped parsley and chopped garlic and some lemon slices.

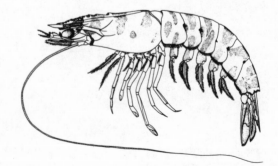

one of the larger
Mediterranean
prawns, Penaeus
kerathurus

CASSOLA DE POP

Cazuela de pulpo   Casserole of octopus

Throughout summer and autumn, octopus are plentiful in the coastal waters, and are easy to catch with a simple fork-like harpoon or even with bare hands. A local newspaper, *Ultima Hora,* is fond of reporting record catches such as 205 in two weeks by a couple of enthusiasts from Barcelona. The pair once took 20 in one hour!

It is common to see fishermen beating octopus against a rock, to help tenderize a creature which tends to be tough and to need prolonged cooking. Large cooked octopus are often seen on fish stalls, and the vendor will cut pieces off for sale, usually to be added to salads.

1 octopus of about 1 kg (2 lb)	1 red pepper, deseeded and roughly chopped
2 tbsp olive oil	2 tbsp finely chopped parsley
1 whole head of garlic, the cloves all peeled	2 tsp mild paprika
4 large Mediterranean spring onions, roughly chopped	dry white wine, as needed salt and black pepper

Wash the octopus in several changes of water and carefully remove its innards, including the ink sac. Cut off the beak and eyes with a knife. Then cut the tentacles and body into pieces of about 3 cm (1").

Heat the oil in a casserole and gently fry the garlic, spring onion, and red pepper in it for about 5 minutes. Add the pieces of octopus, stir in the parsley and paprika and pour over enough white wine just to cover everything. Season with salt and pepper and simmer gently for about an hour.

This casserole dish makes a good first course, served with plenty of bread.

CALAMARS

Calamares   Squid

The small fishing boats or *llauts* that have been adapted for squid fishing are easily recognisable in any of the island's fishing ports, for suspended over the side of each is the large propane-fuelled lamp in whose light the squid are caught at night. I used to believe that when the squid rose to the surface, attracted by the light, they were quickly scooped up in a net. In reality, it is a long, slow process. A small spindle ending in many upturned hooks is lowered into the water and moved slowly up and down. This attracts the squid, whose tentacles become entangled in the hooks and which are thus caught, one by one.

Fresh squid are considered a delicacy by Majorcans and indeed throughout the Mediterranean region. A really fresh specimen can be recognised by the speckled coral-pink tint of the thin skin which covers it. Prolonged storage in ice results in this skin being broken and the colour changing to an unappetizing grey.

Some Majorcans believe that if squid are kept for a day or two after being caught they become more tender and the flavour improves. Be that as it may, all agree that squid will keep well in the refrigerator for up to three days (uncovered, as a covering would cause sweating and deterioration, and anyway they have no fishy smell).

Cleaning squid is easy. Simply hold the body in one hand, and the head and tentacles in the other, and gently pull the head away from the body. With it will come most of the innards, including the ink sac. Remove this carefully, reserving it if your recipe calls for it, and discard the rest of the innards. Rinse out whatever is left inside the body, and pull out the translucent 'bone'. Finally, pull off the thin skin and, if you wish, remove the two triangular flaps (fins) which are attached to the end of the body. Body, head and tentacles are now ready for cooking. (The eyes are still there, but are not eaten).

CALAMARS GROSSOS FARCITS AMB SALSA

Calamares grandes rellenos   Large stuffed squid
con salsa   with a sauce

Occasionally large squid appear in the fish market, some of them weighing 1 kg or more. In May 1986, the newspaper *Ultima Hora* reported the capture of a squid weighing 14 kg by two fishermen off Colonia de Sant Jordi. It was subsequently stuffed and cooked by a local restaurant. The following recipe is one way of dealing with lesser giants.

2 large squid, of not less than 600 g (1 lb 5 oz) each	1 glass dry white wine
200 g (7 oz) minced pork	1 small onion, finely chopped
1 lamb's brain, cut into pieces	1 tbsp pine nuts
1 egg, beaten	a few sprigs of parsley
2 tbsp chopped parsley	1 slice of bread soaked in water
salt and pepper	250 g (9 oz) cooked peas
olive oil	fried bread for garnish

Clean the squid and chop the tentacles finely. Mix these with the minced pork, the lamb's brain, the beaten egg, the parsley and season well. Stuff the body with this mixture and fasten the openings with a toothpick.

Cover the bottom of a frying-pan with oil and heat it. Put in the squid and fry carefully (with a cover on, since they spit), turning frequently until they are golden. Remove them from the frying-pan to an earthenware casserole (*greixonera*). Pour over the dry white wine, bring to the boil and add the oil from the frying-pan and a large glass of water. Simmer slowly for 35 minutes, turning once.

Pound to a paste in a pestle and mortar the chopped onion, pine nuts, sprigs of parsley and the soaked bread, squeezed dry. (If you lack a pestle and mortar, improvise with a bowl and the end of a rolling pin). Season with black pepper and stir in a little stock from the *greixonera*. Remove the squid and add this paste to the casserole together with the cooked peas, stirring well. Bring to the boil and leave to simmer for a few minutes.

147

Meanwhile, cut the squid into thick slices and arrange them on a heated serving dish. Pour the green pea sauce over the top and garnish with triangles of fried bread.

CALAMARS FARCITS

Calamares rellenos   Stuffed squid

Choose equal-size squid weighing about 125-150 g (4-5 oz) each. This recipe does four people as a first course.

8 squid weighing about 1 kg (2 lb) or a little more	2 heaped tbsp fresh breadcrumbs
½ onion, very finely chopped	salt
50 g (2 oz) seedless raisins	freshly ground white pepper
50 g (2 oz) pine nuts	olive oil
2 egg yolks, lightly beaten	1 glass dry white wine

Clean the squid and drop the bodies into a pan of boiling water for a few minutes. Drain and leave to cool.

Cut the tentacles into small pieces and put into a bowl with the onion, raisins, pine nuts, breadcrumbs and the egg yolks. Season and form a paste. Stuff the squid with this mixture and fasten the opening with a toothpick.

In an earthenware casserole (*greixonera*), heat a little olive oil over a low flame. Add the squid and fry lightly and carefully for 10 minutes, turning frequently so that they do not stick to the bottom. Pour in the wine, allow to bubble up, then turn the heat right down and leave to cook slowly, turning occasionally, until the liquid is reduced to almost nothing. Serve the squid hot and dry from the casserole they were cooked in.

CALAMARS FRITS

Calamares fritos   Fried squid

This is the simplest way of cooking squid, common in Majorcan seafood restaurants and very good. Use fresh not frozen squid as the flavour of the latter will not be right.

The head and tentacles of each cleaned squid should first be re-attached to its body with a toothpick, and the whole coated in seasoned flour.

Choose a frying-pan with a lid, large enough to take all the squid side by side, and cover the bottom with olive oil. Heat it over a medium flame, then put in the squid, which will sizzle on contact with the hot oil. Cover at once, to protect yourself and your kitchen from their spitting.

Keep the squid sizzling briskly for a few seconds then turn the heat down and fry gently for 5 minutes. Remove the pan from the heat and carefully take off the lid. Turn the squid over. The underneath part should be golden brown. Add two whole unpeeled garlic cloves per squid to the pan. Return to the heat and cover. Again cook on a medium to high flame for a few seconds, then reduce the heat and cook for another 5 minutes or until golden brown. Serve with the pan juices poured over and plenty of fresh bread to mop them up. I like to serve the whole garlic cloves too.

Two average sized squid, of about 150 g (5 oz) each, uncleaned weight, make a helping for one person.

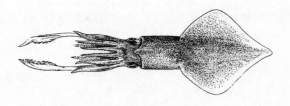

a squid of the species Loligo vulgaris

CALAMARINS I SIPIOLES

Calamarines y chipirones

Baby squid and tiny cuttlefish

The little squid I refer to are babies which would grow much larger. The tiny cuttlefish, on the other hand, belong to the species *Sepiola* (shown in the drawing) and *Rossia,* and never grow more than 3-4 cm (1-1½"), whereas the regular cuttlefish. *Sepia officinalis,* can be much bigger. Anyway, these are all such small creatures that it's usual not to fiddle about cleaning them but to cook them as they are. They are utterly delicious and well worth the high price they fetch.

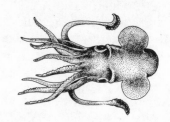

The simplest thing to do with them is to rinse them, pat them dry, dust them lightly with seasoned flour, then deep fry them in olive oil until golden and crisp. Serve with wedges of lemon, and bread, at the start of a meal.

But here is another way, used by a chef at the Club de Vela in Puerto de Andraitx to prepare evening *tapas,* out of the tourist season, for regular customers at the bar.

1 kg (2 lb) baby squid or tiny cuttlefish
250 ml (9 fl oz) olive oil
3 onions, finely chopped
2 tbsp finely chopped parsley
2 cloves garlic, finely chopped
salt and black pepper
a pinch or two of ground cinnamon

Rinse and pat dry the small squid (or cuttlefish). Heat the oil in a frying-pan and add the onion, frying gently until soft, then add the remaining ingredients plus the prepared squid. Stir, and add a tablespoon or two of water, to ensure that they are moist when served. Cook gently until the squid are tender — about 10-15 minutes.

150

MUSCLOS

Mejillones   Mussels

Majorcan mussels are inexpensive and available all year round. The Spanish, who are by far the greatest producers of 'farmed' mussels in Europe, do not follow the old British rule of marketing mussels only when there is an 'r' in the month. This is probably a hangover from the days when farming and transportation methods were less advanced and it was advisable to avoid mussels in the hot summer months, when they could easily be contaminated. They are perfectly safe to eat in the 'r'-less summer months if you follow three basic rules.

First, buy mussels from a reputable source with a brisk turnover. Second, cook them within 24 hours of purchase. And last, be sure to clean them thoroughly.

Wash the mussels well in cold running water, discarding any with broken shells. Now put them in a sink or bowl full of cold water and discard any that float on the surface. (When dealing with any shellfish, 'if in doubt, throw out' is the best policy). With a sharp knife, remove the 'beard' and any growths on the shell. Rinse again in cold water.

Once the mussels are cleaned, put them in a single or double layer in a wide saucepan over a low heat. Cover with a lid and shake the pan occasionally. The mussels will open in the steam. Remove the lid as they begin to open (some take longer than others) and shake the pan well. Take out the mussels as they open (a moist and juicy freshly opened mussel would soon become shrivelled and rubbery if left in the pan). Any mussels that fail to open after reasonable exposure to heat, discard. When the cooking liquid has cooled, pour some of it over the cooked mussels to keep them moist.

Served alone or sprinkled with a little lemon juice, these mussels make an excellent starter. Or, after allowing them to cool and removing the empty half shells, the mussels can be spread on top with a mixture of mayonnaise and finely chopped spring onion — these are popular *tapas*.

151

Poultry and Game

Keeping poultry, usually chickens and turkeys, is still fairly common in the rural areas of Majorca, but fewer and fewer families now bother with the extra work involved in maintaining rabbits, ducks, pigeons or pheasants for the table. Yet, within living memory this was once a way of life; if you lived in a town, you bought your poultry and rabbits live from the markets. In the days before refrigeration, keeping meat for even a short time in a warm climate was a recognisable health hazard. Nowadays, with full refrigeration and modern farming methods, fresh poultry, rabbit and pigeon are more conveniently bought ready for cooking.

You can also find quail, which were once quite a rarity, since they stop on the island only briefly on their migratory journey from Africa. Now they are extensively farmed and have become very popular in *tapas* bars, in restaurants and in the home. An added bonus is that quails' eggs are cheap and plentiful.

The yellow corn-fed Spanish chickens make the British ones look anaemic. Spanish chickens have a taste and flavour almost forgotten in Britain; this is due mainly to more natural farming methods, which also mean they have less fat. They are an excellent buy. But one word of warning: though rabbits, pigeons and quails are sold oven-ready, this is not always the case with chickens, ducks and turkeys. If you buy one of these birds from a butcher's shop, the butcher (probably a woman) will produce the whole bird, including head and feet, which she will then clean and prepare for you, asking if you want the bird whole or cut into pieces, and offering the head, feet and giblets (which be sure to accept — they are useful for stock). If, on the other hand, you buy your bird at a supermarket, it will come in a plastic tray, wrapped in cling film and will look oven-ready. In fact, its feet, head and giblets will still be there and you have to remove them yourself. I have met many people who have carefully removed the head and feet and cooked the bird without realising until too late that the giblets were still inside.

PHEASANT AND PARTRIDGE

Some old habits die hard. While still new to the island, I spent a large sum of money on a brace of pheasants for a special *fiesta* dinner. The Majorcan idea of a brace was two males, frozen stiff in all their feathered glory. Realizing, when I had defrosted them, that they had not been hung, I asked my Majorcan friends how long I should hang them before cooking. I thought that the length of time would be different in a mild Mediterranean winter climate. They were horrified by my question; and so was I for that matter, when I realised that game is not hung in Majorca but eaten as soon as possible.

I was also somewhat horrified to discover the way in which the pheasant is presented for sale. Indiscriminate hunting has wiped out the wild pheasant, so the birds are now farmed for the table. Once killed, they are sent immediately to market, where they are held, fully feathered, in a chill cabinet or a deep freeze until sold. They are especially popular and in plentiful supply over the Christmas period. In supermarkets, they are shoved into individual plastic mesh bags and piled up for sale in an open display refrigerator.

There are no licensed game dealers. The pheasant, once bought and quickly plucked, would find its way into a *paella, arroz brut* or some kind of stew, the only ways to cook what will prove to be a tough bird.

The indiscriminate hunting that saw off the wild pheasant has also affected the hare. This used to be very plentiful and it features in many old local recipes; but it is now rarely on sale and appears only in the most expensive of restaurants. Wild rabbit makes an occasional appearance at the game stall upstairs in the Olivar market in Palma, but it is the red-legged partridge which affords the only real hunting available on the island. This is carried out with great enthusiasm, though subject these days to strict control. There is a breeding programme to release partridge into the wild to maintain numbers. Like pheasant, the partridges are not normally hung, so Majorcan recipes for them tend to be the stew type. The unhung bird, unless very young, will be tough. I have not included any specific pheasant or partridge recipes here for that reason.

SMALL BIRDS

As in many other European countries, such as Italy, small birds are classed as game, and the thrush, a great favourite with the Majorcans, is the most common of these. They are caught traditionally by netting, though many are shot.

One February, when out gathering wild asparagus, I climbed a dry stone wall to get into a field where I could see a profusion of prickly asparagus bushes. Baltazar suddenly cautioned me to watch where I was treading — there were some mounds of freshly dug earth with a maggot on the tip. Avoiding these and walking on, I saw that they were bird traps; a robin and a sparrow were ensnared, dead, in a couple of them. Attracted to the maggots, they had landed to peck at them and were caught by the mouse-trap action of the trap concealed under the earth. This is an illegal method of catching birds — the victims were for eating — and is not often seen.

The thrushes start to arrive from colder northern parts in October; the season begins then and continues to the end of January. If it is a good season, thrushes are usually available from several stalls in the upstairs butchers' section in the Olivar market in Palma. For a few pesetas more you can buy the thrushes plucked though undrawn. They do not need to be hung and have a distinctive but not gamey flavour.

ESCALDUMS DE POLLASTRE (O D'INDIOT)

Guison de pollo   Fricassee of chicken
(o pavo)   (or turkey)

A popular *fiesta* dish, especially over the Christmas and New Year holidays. Frankly, you will wonder why, if you ever try the standard restaurant version of *escaldums* — usually a dull, unimaginative chicken or turkey stew served with soggy roast potatoes.

My recipe is based on that in *Cocina Selecta Mallorquina* by the venerable Sra Abrines Vidal. If you opt for turkey, buy pieces adding up to the weight specified for the chicken.

1 chicken weighing about	1 bay leaf
1½ kg (3 lb 5 oz)	1 tsp dried oregano
25 g (1 oz) lard	100 ml (3½ fl oz) dry
1 tbsp olive oil	white wine
1 onion, very finely sliced	¼ litre (9 fl oz) water
1 whole head garlic	30 g (1 oz) whole blanched
1 large ripe tomato of about	almonds
200 g (7 oz), skinned	a small piece of *sobrasada*
and chopped	milk as required

Cut the chicken into neat, small pieces, removing all the skin and as many of the bones as possible. Heat the lard and the olive oil together in a saucepan and gently fry the chicken pieces until they are a golden colour, then remove them from the pan with a slotted spoon.

Now add the sliced onion to the remaining fat. When the onion has softened, add the garlic cloves, lightly crushed but whole and unpeeled; the tomato; the bay leaf and oregano; and the white wine and water. Return the chicken pieces to the pan and bring to the boil. Simmer, covered, for 40 minutes. (If possible at this stage, leave the *escaldums* overnight for the dish will taste much better. The next day, bring it back to the boil and continue with the recipe). Fry the almonds in a little olive oil until golden, pound them in a mortar with the *sobrasada,* adding a few drops of water to make a good paste. Thin this paste with a little milk, add it to the chicken, simmer for 10 minutes and then serve with the traditional accompaniment of small, round roast potatoes (not soggy, as in the restaurants!).

GALLINA TRUFADA

Gallina trufada   Truffled hen

A Majorcan party dish; it is served cold and cut into thin slices as a *fiambre* (cold cut), though it is just as good hot. Chicken tends to be substituted for hen these days. The truffles (which are sold in little bottles) are sometimes omitted; pine nuts and raisins, about a tablespoon each, can be used instead.

1 fat hen, boned	2 tbsp brandy
¼ kg (9 oz) minced beef	100 g (3½ oz) ham
¼ kg (9 oz) minced pork	100 g (3½ oz) bacon
salt	2 truffles
½ nutmeg, grated	50 g (2 oz) lard
freshly ground black pepper	100 ml (3½ fl oz) dry
1 egg	sherry

Mix the two kinds of minced meat together and season with salt, nutmeg and plenty of black pepper. Stir in the beaten egg and brandy. Cut the ham and bacon into slices and the truffles into rounds. (If you are substituting pine nuts and raisins, mix these in with the minced meat). Stuff the boned hen or chicken with alternate layers of the minced meat mixture and the slices of bacon and ham. Arrange the truffles in such a way that when the bird is sliced they will be fairly evenly distributed.

Sew or tie the hen into shape and place it in a roasting tin into which it just fits. Spread the lard over it and pour the sherry and the same amount of water into the roasting tin. Bake, uncovered, at 200°C (390°F/gas mark 5) for 1¼ hours, basting frequently. Serve hot or cold.

PITERA DE POLLASTRE FARCIDA

Pechuga de pollo rellena	Stuffed breast of chicken
4 large chicken breasts	½ apple, peeled and
for the stuffing	finely diced
100 g (5 oz) minced pork	2 slices of bread, soaked
50 g (2 oz) *sobrasada*	in milk and squeezed dry
50 g (2 oz) *jamón serrano,* or	salt
good quality ham or	¼ tsp each of ground
bacon, finely diced	cloves, cinnamon,
1 egg yolk	nutmeg, cumin seed,
	white pepper

Mix all the above ingredients, except the chicken breasts, together. Cover part of your work surface with cling film, arrange the chicken breasts on top and cover with more cling film. Beat the breasts flat with a rolling pin, season them with salt and pepper, and spread the prepared stuffing on top. Then roll each chicken breast up like a thick sausage. Wrap and seal each one well with greased baking foil.

for the casserole	1 bay leaf
25 g (1 oz) lard	100 ml (3 ½ fl oz) of
1 carrot, 1 onion, 1 leek	brandy
and 1 stick celery all cut	100 ml (3 ½ fl oz) of
into pieces, together with	dry sherry
1 large ripe tomato, skinned	8 pitted prunes
and chopped	8 dried apricots
½ tsp dried thyme	25 g (1 oz) pine nuts

In a casserole, preferably of earthenware (a *greixonera*), heat the lard and soften the vegetables in it. Then add all the other ingredients, except the pine nuts.

Cover the casserole (with foil if it has no lid), and put it on the middle shelf of your (preheated) oven. Place the wrapped chicken breasts on the top shelf. Bake at 200°C (390°F, gas mark 5) for 45 minutes.

Now remove everything from the oven. Take out the prunes and apricots from the casserole. Pass the remaining sauce through a vegetable mill or liquidise it in a blender. Return it to the cleaned casserole and add the pine nuts, pounded to a paste in a mortar. Stir, then return the prunes and apricots to the sauce.

Remove the chicken breasts from the foil, cut them into thick slices, and arrange these on top of the casserole. Heat through and serve at once.

CROQUETES DE GALLINA

Croquetas de gallina   Chicken croquettes

Croquettes of chicken or seafood make popular *tapas* or a light main course. They are one of the few convenience foods available in Majorca, ready made and frozen, requiring only thawing and deep-frying. But, like almost all foods, they are much better home-made; and they are a convenient way of using up left-over cooked chicken or fish.

1 small onion, minced	1 tbsp chopped parsley
25 g (1 oz) lard	2 egg yolks (reserve the
25 g (1 oz) flour	whites)
¼ litre (9 fl oz) chicken	salt and pepper
stock	1 more egg
150 g (5 oz) cooked chicken,	breadcrumbs as required
finely chopped	oil for deep frying
50 g (2 oz) *sobrasada,*	
skinned and chopped	

Fry the onions in the lard until just starting to take colour and stir in the flour. Whisk in the hot meat stock and simmer on a low heat, stirring frequently, for 10 minutes. Then mix in the chicken, *sobrasada* and parsley, and remove from the heat. Beat in the egg yolks and season well. Pour onto a dinner plate and leave to cool.

Now shape the mixture into about 12 croquettes. Lightly beat the egg whites with the third egg and dip the croquettes in this mixture, then roll them in the breadcrumbs until completely covered. Deep fry in hot oil until golden.

SALSA D'AMETTLES

Salsa de almendras   Almond sauce for poultry and game

Perhaps because they are easy and quick to cook, tiny baby chickens (*picantones*), the size of pigeons and packed, oven ready, in threes, or the larger spring chicken (*coquelet*) are now always available at the hypermarkets and some supermarkets. They go extremely well with this almond sauce, which is a variation of the sauce in the *capirotada* recipe (p 162). It also makes a pleasant alternative to the usual *allioli* or garlic mayonnaise that goes with charcoal-grilled rabbit.

100 g (3 ½ oz) blanched
   whole almonds
2 peeled garic cloves

1 cooked egg yolk
¼ litre (9 fl oz) meat
   stock
salt

Pound in a mortar, or (better) grind in an electric blender, the almonds, garlic and egg yolk and place the resulting paste in a saucepan. Whisk in the hot stock. Heat slowly on top of the stove, stirring all the time, for about 5 minutes, until the sauce is thick and creamy.

CONILL AMB CEBA

Conejo con cebolla   Rabbit with onions

1 rabbit
25 g (1 oz) *sobrasada*
100 g (3 ½ oz) bacon

4 tbsp olive oil
700 g (1 lb 9 oz) onion
2 tbsp brandy

Fry the *sobrasada* and the bacon slices until all the fat has run from both and they are crisp and coloured. Remove and discard them.

    Cut the rabbit into pieces (though I never include the rib cage, using it instead for stock), and fry these in the flavoured fat until golden. Remove them from the frying-pan and reserve on a plate.

    Now add the olive oil to the pan and the onion, sliced into very fine rings. Fry over a high flame until the onion has taken on a golden brown colour.

Place the rabbit and its juices (which will have collected on the plate), together with the onion, in a deep earthenware casserole. Pour in the brandy and just a little water or good meat stock. Cover and simmer on top of the stove for one hour.

Just before serving, season with a little ground cinnamon, clove and black pepper and salt. The rabbit should be tender with just a small amount of rich, brown sauce thickened with the onions.

This makes 2 large portions.

CONILL ESCABETX

Conejo en escabeche   Marinated rabbit

1 rabbit
1 large onion, finely
   sliced
1 whole head garlic
8 peppercorns
a small stick of cinnamon

225 ml (8 fl oz) olive oil
75 ml (3 fl oz) white
   wine vinegar
salt

Cut the rabbit into manageable pieces. Place these in a deep earthenware pot, if possible — otherwise an ordinary oven-proof casserole. Separate and peel the garlic cloves. Cover the rabbit with these, the onion, peppercorns, cinnamon and salt. Pour on the oil and vinegar. Leave to marinate for at least 24 hours.

Bring to a simmer on top of the stove, then cover tightly with a lid or foil and transfer to a moderate oven (180°C/355°F/gas mark 4) for 1 hour. Serve hot with potatoes or rice, and pour a little of the marinade over them.

This dish keeps for some time under refrigeration and reheats well. The rabbit itself is very tender and sweet.

This recipe makes 2 large portions.

CAPIROTADA DE CONILL (O POLLASTRE)

Capirotada de conejo   'Capirotada' of rabbit
(o pollo)   (or chicken)

Although this dish is eminently suitable for a boiling fowl, mature rabbits or the tough Majorcan pheasants and partridges, it is now more common to make *capirotada* with the more tender roasting chicken and young rabbit. If you wish to prepare the cheaper mature poultry and game in this manner, the simmering time should be longer.

1 large rabbit or chicken	50 g (2 oz) lard
1 onion, roughly sliced	1 thick slice white bread
2 carrots, roughly sliced	100 g (3 ½ oz) blanched
8 whole peppercorns	whole almonds
2 whole cloves	salt and pepper
1 bay leaf	1 small stick of cinnamon

Quarter the chicken or rabbit and place in a saucepan with the onion, carrots, peppercorns, cloves and bay leaf. Cover with water and simmer for about 40 minutes or until the meat is tender. Strain off and reserve the liquid, but discard the vegetables and spices and leave the meat until it is cool enough to handle. Then cut it into large pieces, removing all skin and bone.

Fry the slice of bread in the lard and grind it in a blender (or use pestle and mortar) with the almonds. Skim the fat from the surface of the reserved stock and slowly stir ¼ litre (9 fl oz) into a saucepan with the bread and almonds. Add the seasoning and the cinnamon. Bring slowly to the boil, then simmer very gently, stirring frequently, for 5 minutes — the sauce will become thick and creamy.

Meanwhile, fry the meat in the remaining lard until golden; arrange it on a heated serving plate and keep it warm. Fry triangles of bread, using extra lard if necessary, and put these round the serving dish as garnish. Remove the stick of cinnamon from the sauce, which is passed round separately.

I hope that someone, some day, will finally clear up the mysterious history of the name *capirotada*. An inconclusive discussion in the Prospect Books journal, *PPC,* suggests that it first meant a sauce, of variable composition, but then came to mean a savoury dish incorporating such a sauce (as here). But in New Mexico it has emerged as a sweet pudding!

TORDS O COLOMINS AMB COL

Tordos o pichones	Thrushes or pigeons
con col	with cabbage

Tordos con col, thrushes wrapped in cabbage leaves, is the most popular of the Majorcan thrush dishes, and during the short winter season is offered in many restaurants, pigeon or sometimes quail taking over at other times. Allow 2 thrushes or 1 pigeon per person.

In a saucepan of boiling water put in the same number of large, perfect cabbage leaves, without their stems, as there are birds to be wrapped, and blanch them for 4 minutes. Drain them and spread them out on the work surface.

Heat 25 g (1 oz) lard in a frying-pan and lightly brown the cleaned birds. Place one bird on top of each cabbage leaf and inside the gut cavity place a little *sobrasada,* some very thin slices of *butifarron* and 2 tiny pieces of pork loin. On either side of the bird, place a slice of *butifarron* and a slice of pork loin. Wrap each bird up in its cabbage leaf like a parcel.

To cook 8 thrush parcels, or 4 pigeons, heat 25 g (1 oz) lard in an earthenware casserole. Finely chop a large onion and gently fry it. Once it is soft, add 1 large peeled and chopped tomato, a dessertspoon of vinegar, ½ teaspoon of oregano, and a tablespoon of finely chopped parsley. Simmer for a few minutes, then add the cabbage parcels. After turning these over a few times in the sauce, for a couple of minutes only, add just enough water to cover the cabbage, cover the casserole and leave it to simmer for 1 hour.

Serve with fried potatoes.

GUATLERES AMB PILOTES

Cordonices con albondigas   Quails with meatballs

A recipe for 4 people from Restaurante Celler Ca Vostra in Puerto de Pollensa. They presented this dish at the First Exhibition of Majorcan Cookery in Palma in 1985.

4 quails
200 g (7 oz) minced pork
¼ tsp ground nutmeg
¼ tsp black pepper
¼ tsp dried oregano
¼ tsp dried mint
¼ tsp ground cinnamon
salt
1 egg, beaten
olive oil
1 large onion, finely
  chopped

2 large, ripe tomatoes,
  skinned and chopped
potatoes, as required
¼ litre (9 fl oz) meat
  stock
setas (wild mushrooms) or
  cultivated mushrooms
1 tbsp finely chopped
  parsley
2 cloves of garlic, finely
  chopped
1 tbsp vinegar
salt

Combine the minced pork with the nutmeg, pepper, oregano, mint and cinnamon. Add a little salt and mix in the beaten egg. Roll into meatballs about the size of walnuts, using a little flour to help form them if necessary.

Heat plenty of oil in a large frying-pan and fry the meatballs until golden brown. Remove from the pan with a slotted spoon and reserve on a plate. Add the whole quails to the remaining oil and fry until brown all over. Remove and set them aside with the meatballs.

Using the same oil, fry the onion until transparent. Stir in the tomatoes and cook gently for 10 minutes. Arrange the quails and the meatballs in a casserole with enough peeled and diced potatoes for 4 people. Pour in the meat stock and add some *setas* or mushrooms, keeping them whole if possible. Simmer gently for 30-40 minutes. Add the chopped parsley and garlic mixed with the vinegar, just before serving.

CARAGOLS

Caracoles   Snails

The esteem with which the Majorcans regard snails, together with their enthusiasm for gathering wild ones after the spring and autumn rains, has often made me feel surprised that there are still any left to gather. Though they can be bought occasionally at the Oilvar and Santa Catalina markets in Palma, collecting your own snails is normal; and since you 'hunt' them I have counted them as 'game'.

Majorcans look for two types of edible snail: the very large *bover* and the small *viuda,* both with circular shells and pronounced tabby markings. Some Majorcan recipes refer directly to the snail by these names but I prefer to use the small *viuda* at all times as I find the *bover* rather too larger-than-life for my liking. They are best collected at night, after a fall of rain, when the snails are at their most active. With the help of a powerful lamp, they can be found along the sides of country roads and in the vegetation and stone walls bordering fields. Some can still be found during the day, again after a good fall of rain.

Advice from enthusiasts on the proper way to deal with snails can be varied and somewhat confusing, as everyone seems to have their own personal method of keeping and cleaning them and cookery books on the subject are not much help. Several in my collection say that the snails must be kept without food for one month before cooking them. Apparently, this is the only way to ensure that they are properly cleaned. Now I would never bother to go snail-hunting after the first heavy rain of late summer for the snails are so wasted away and tasteless after starving all summer long that they need a course of fattening before they are ready to be eaten. I am therefore not willingly going to starve to nothing plump, well-fed snails. 24 hours is sufficient to clean a snail but to be on the safe side I usually keep them for 3 days, 6 days at most, otherwise they begin to lose their plumpness.

This method, which I learnt in a restaurant, is the best way to deal with snails. Once collected, give them a quick rinse in

165

cold running water to remove superfluous soil, grit and vegetation, and then place them in a bucket or bowl with a cloth tied over the top. Keep this in a cool spot overnight. The next day, rinse the snails again and put them back in the bucket with a layer of flour in the bottom for them to eat. The action of the flour removes all grit from their digestive tract and cleans them out thoroughly.* After this, leave them in a cool, dark spot for about three days. Then wash and wash the snails in cold running water until the water runs clear.

As the snails start to come out of their shells and move again after all the washing, pick them out of the sink and place them in a saucepan; discard any shells that show no movement. The live snails are then covered with water and this is brought very slowly to the boil. It seems to have a soporific effect on the snails and they remain outside their shells making them easy to extract for eating; if they were plunged into boiling water or brought to the boil too quickly, they would retract at once. Simmer for 10 minutes, then drain off the water, which will contain a lot of scum.

Wash the snails once again in cold running water and put them back in the cleaned saucepan. Cover again with cold water and bring quickly to the boil, then lower the heat and put in a big bunch of fresh herbs which you can either buy from the markets or put together yourself. In spring the bunch should consist of lots of fresh green fennel leaves (which can be collected anywhere on the island), some fresh oregano, fresh mint, fresh parsley and a stick or two of celery; in late summer and autumn the bunch should contain lots of fennel stalks and heads, fresh mint, fresh parsley and celery. Add some salt also, and simmer for 2 hours. Then remove from the heat and continue with the recipe on the next page.

---

*I was interested to see that Patience Gray's meticulous description, in *Honey from a Weed,* of the preparation of snails in Apulia also involves flour.

CARAGOLS AMB SALSA

Caracoles en salsa   Snails in a sauce

Snails are always served as a starter in restaurants and Majorcan homes, and this dish is no exception.

500 g (1 lb) cooked snails,
  with their cooking liquid
2 tbsp olive oil
1 large onion, finely
  chopped
250 g (8 oz) very ripe
  tomatoes, peeled and
  chopped

4 cloves of garlic, finely
  chopped
2 tbsp finely chopped
  parsley
100 g (3½ oz) *jamón serrano*
  or other good ham,
  diced
salt
freshly ground black pepper

In a casserole, preferably of earthenware, heat the olive oil and soften the onion in it, without letting it start to colour. Add the tomatoes and the garlic, and simmer until the tomatoes have formed a thick sauce.

Now stir in the chopped parsley, and add the diced ham and the snails. Cover with some of the snails' cooking liquid and simmer for half an hour. Adjust the seasoning, grinding in some black pepper; salt may not be necessary as the ham can often be salty enough.

Serve piping hot in bowls with crusty bread, wooden tooth-picks to extract the snails and garlic mayonnaise in a separate bowl.

To this basic recipe, you could add, with the ham and the snails, finely diced potatoes, broad beans, green beans, a little *sobrasada* or a few slices of diced *butifarra*. And a *picada* made from a handful of blanched whole almonds, pounded in a mortar with a handful of roughly chopped parsley, is sometimes added to the dish 10 minutes before serving.

Meat

Majorcan cookery makes the most of an animal: nothing is wasted. A stroll around the enormous meat section of the Olivar market in central Palma will reveal heads, tails, innards, feet and even blood for sale. Growing prosperity has not dampened the Majorcan enthusiasm for the cheaper parts of the animal. The heart, lungs and liver of a pig or lamb, tripe and kidneys all make *tapas*. Heads, feet, ears and bones are utilised in the very popular bean soups or *potajes*. Majorcan recipes often combine cuts of varying price for taste and textural contrasts. For example smooth pork fat, *tocina,* is cooked with fibrous lamb, pork or beef; and belly pork, *panceta,* is frequently added to stewing meat.

The lengthy hanging of meat to age and tenderise it was, until recently, impossible in Mediterranean countries. As with poultry and game, the quicker the meat was eaten, the better. This is probably why lamb and pigs are killed at a much younger age than in Britain. The tender young cuts were perfect for roasting and grilling. Meat from the mature cows, pigs and sheep would have been for long, slow stewing.

Although many Spanish cookery books give the impression that their regional meat cookery is nothing but stews, this is only because the roasting and grilling of meat requires little direction. Many excellent Majorcan dishes are roast or grilled meat; leg or shoulder of lamb, whole baby lamb, suckling pig or tender chops or steaks from these animals, which require nothing more than the pan juices they were cooked in and a little lemon juice.

The recipes in this long chapter start with those which are of a general character or for mixed meats; then come beef recipes (from page 179), followed by those for pork (from page 185) and lamb (from page 192).

BULLIT

Cocido   Mixed boiled meats and vegetables

A close relation of the French *pot-au-feu* and the Italian *bollito misto, bullit* appears so regularly on the lunch tables of Majorcan homes that it could claim to be Majorca's national dish*. Yet the only time I have seen it served in a restaurant was when the staff sat down to eat it for their lunch. It is thought of as very much a domestic dish. However, I have since discovered that it occasionally appears on the menu of Ca'n Nofre, at Heroes de Manacor 27, Palma, one of the most highly regarded Mallorquin restaurants.

It is, in fact, two dishes. Various meats and vegetables are slowly simmered in a large pot of either earthenware or metal. The broth is then strained off and pasta or rice added to it. This soup is served as the first course; the meat and vegetables are the main course. The ingredients for *bullit* are as varied as the methods for preparing it; each household seems to have a different system. The accompanying vegetables change with the season but, in general, *bullit* always contains potatoes and cabbage. Beef and poultry are a popular combination, but if cooking for a large number, lamb and pork can be added as well. The recipe on the next page is for 6-8 people.

*In saying this, I do not intend to tread on the toes of people on the mainland of Spain, who take pride in their *cocido,* and might indeed claim that it was one of their national dishes. Alicia Rios delivered a remarkably poetic and philosophical paper on the subject at the 1984 Oxford Symposia on Food History (subsequently printed in issue 18 of the Prospect Books journal, *PPC*), exploring what she calls the 'typology' of the *cocido* as well as its history and nutritional qualities. She laments its evolution from being daily nourishment for the poor (among whom one ham-bone would be passed from household to household, flavouring numerous *cocidos* in turn) to being a luxury dish for special occasions. It seems that in mainland Spain the pressures of life have been edging it out of the home and onto restaurant menus; whereas, as I remark above, *bullit* is still essentially a domestic dish in Majorca.

400-500 g (about 1 lb) beef,
  in one piece (*redondo de
  ternera*)
1 marrow bone
150 g (5 oz) pork fat,
  (*tocino*)
1 small *butifarra* or *camaiot*
  (about 450 g / 1 lb)
1 boiling fowl (*gallina*)
500 g (1 lb) potatoes, peeled
250 g (8 oz) sweet potatoes
  (if available)
500 g (1 lb) white cabbage,
  quartered

12-16 small onions or
  shallots, peeled
whole seasonal vegetables
  e g mange-tout, green
  beans, carrots, leeks
  etc, to be cooked
  separately and served
  with the meat (these are
  optional)
100 g (3 ½ oz) medium
  grain rice or small
  shaped pasta
1 tsp mild paprika
salt and pepper

Put the beef, marrow bone and pork fat into a large saucepan and cover with cold water. Bring very slowly to the boil, skimming off the scum as soon as it starts to rise. It will probably continue rising for 10 minutes or so and all must be skimmed away. When the scum becomes a thin white foam, it can be left. Add the *butifarra* or *camaiot* and season. Cover, and simmer gently for one hour. Then add the boiling fowl, kept whole, and simmer for a further hour or so; but take care not to let the fowl fall to pieces.

Meanwhile, set the potatoes and cabbage to cook in a separate saucepan with the onions and seasoning. If using the other (optional) vegetables, cook them in a further pan, starting with the vegetables that require the longest cooking time and adding the others when necessary.

Strain off just enough broth from the meat to make the soup. Bring it to the boil, adding the rice or pasta and the paprika. Simmer until the rice or pasta is cooked. Serve as the first course.

The meat will have stayed hot in the remaining liquid — it will in fact stay so for up to an hour. Carve the beef and fowl, slice the *butifarra* or *camaiot* and the pork fat and arrange on a warm serving dish with all the vegetables. Dress with a sprinkling of wine vinegar and good quality virgin olive oil, then serve it all as the next course.

MOTLE DE CARN

Molde de carne hervida   Meat mould

There is nearly always meat left over from *bullit*. This is one of many recipes for using it up.

200 g (7 oz) cooked meat
   left over from *bullit*
½ kg (1 lb) aubergines
   sliced
½ kg (1 lb) green or red
   peppers

oil for frying
1 kg (2 ¼ lb) potatoes,
   peeled and sliced
4 eggs
100 ml (3 ½ oz) milk
salt and pepper

Sprinkle the aubergines with salt and leave them to drain in a colander weighted down with a plate for half an hour.

Grill or bake the peppers until the skin is blistered and black, then plunge them into cold water and remove the fine, papery outer skin. Cut the flesh into pieces and discard the seeds.

Fry the sliced potatoes until soft and then the rinsed, sliced aubergines until golden.

Slice the meat, and beat the eggs with the milk and a little seasoning.

Grease an ovenproof dish with oil and put in, in layers, half the potatoes, then all the aubergines, next the peppers, followed by the meat and finally the rest of the potatoes. Season each layer well. Now pour on the egg mixture and bake in a moderate oven at (180°C/355°F/gas mark 4) for 20 minutes.

Turn out onto a serving dish and serve at once with tomato sauce (p 49).

PILOTES AMB SALSA DE JULIVERT

Albondigas con salsa *de perejil*	Meatballs with parsley sauce
600 g (1 ¼ lb) minced beef	1 tbsp chopped parsley
80 g (3 oz) finely chopped ham	2 eggs, beaten salt
50 g (2 oz) finely chopped bacon	white pepper 100 g (3 ½ oz) flour
1 clove garlic, finely chopped	100 ml (3 ½ fl oz) olive oil parsley sauce
1 onion, finely chopped	

Mix the minced beef, ham and bacon together. Add the garlic, onion, parsley and eggs. Season the mixture with salt and white pepper and then, using the flour, form it into meatballs the size of walnuts.

Heat the oil and fry the meatballs until they are golden. Place in a casserole and pour on the parsley sauce (below). Bring to the boil, simmer for 5 minutes and serve.

SALSA DE JULIVERT

Salsa de perejil	Parsley sauce
100 g (3 ½ oz) fresh breadcrumbs	1 heaped tbsp finely chopped parsley
½ - ¾ litre (18-27 fl oz) good meat stock	50 g (2 oz) hazelnuts or almonds, skinned and finely chopped

Soak the breadcrumbs in a little stock, then mix in the parsley, nuts and the rest of the stock. Heat slowly over a low flame, stirring, until the sauce has thickened somewhat, but not too much — to go well with the meatballs, it should not be too thick, and you may find it necessary to add a little more stock to ensure this.

173

ROLLO PINYONAT

Rollo de carne con piñones   Meatloaf with pine nuts

800 g (1 ¾ lb) minced meat
  (*una mezcla*, a mixture —
  half beef, half pork)
100 ml (3 ½ fl oz) dry
  sherry
2 egg yolks
1 heaped tbsp flour

1 tbsp finely chopped onion
1 tsp ground nutmeg
50 g (2 oz) *sobrasada*,
  cut into pieces
salt and pepper
olive oil, to grease the loaf
  tin
50 g (2 oz) pine nuts

Mix the minced meat with the sherry, the beaten egg yolks, half
the flour, the onion, ground nutmeg and *sobrasada* cut into
pieces. Season with salt and pepper.

With the help of the rest of the flour form the meat with your
hands into a ball and then press this into a well-greased loaf tin.
Press the pine nuts onto the top and cover lightly with foil.

Bake in the centre of the oven at a temperature of 190°C
(355°F/gas mark 4) for one hour, then remove the foil and bake
for a further 20-30 minutes, keeping an eye on the pine nuts to
check that they do not burn. Remove from the oven and cool
slightly. Turn out onto a plate and serve, sliced, with the
following sauce.

SALSA DE PINYONS

Salsa de piñones   Pine nut sauce

Pound 100 g (3 ½ oz) of pine nuts in a pestle and mortar with 2
peeled garlic cloves and the hard-boiled yolk of one egg. Place
in a saucepan and stir in ¼ litre (9 fl oz) meat stock and heat
through for a few minutes before serving.

The sauce will thicken slightly but not as much as the almond
sauce (p 160) of which it is a variation. Hazelnuts or walnuts can
also be substituted.

LLENGUA AMB TÀPERES

Lengua con alcaparras   Tongue with caper sauce

This is a well-known Majorcan dish combining cheap, easily obtained tongue with one of the island's main crops, capers.

The recipe on the following two pages, for *Estofado de lengua*, explains how to cook a calf's tongue of about 1 kg (2¼ lb). In the present recipe, I assume that the preliminaries have been carried out and the cooking liquid has been reserved.

1 cooked calf's tongue of about 1 kg (2¼ lb)
75 ml (3 fl oz) olive oil
100 g (3½ oz) *jamón serrano*, cut into small pieces
½ onion, finely chopped
200 g (7 oz) ripe tomatoes, peeled and pulped
10 g (½ oz) hazelnuts

10 g (½ oz) almonds
3 cloves garlic
a few sprigs parsley
1 tbsp flour, carefully toasted in the oven
25 g (1 oz) capers
grated nutmeg
salt
pepper

Heat the oil in a casserole and lightly fry the *jamón serrano*. Add the onion and fry it until it is soft but has not started to colour. Then stir in about ¼ litre (9 fl oz) of the cooking liquid and the tomatoes and simmer gently for 10 minutes.

Meanwhile, pound the hazelnuts and almonds in a mortar with the garlic and parsley. Add the toasted flour and moisten with some of the cooking liquid to form a paste. Stir all this into the consistency of a sauce, season it with the grated nutmeg, salt and pepper, and add the capers.

Cut the tongue into slices and add it to the sauce. Heat through and serve at once.

ESTOFAT DE LLENGUA

Estofado de lengua   Stewed tongue

Fresh tongues, whether the large ones from calves or the smaller pigs' tongues, are available from all butchers' shops in Majorca.

I have never seen any pickled tongues on sale, the usual way they are sold in England. Part of the pickling process involves the use of saltpetre which gives the English tongue its characteristic rich, deep red colour. In contrast, the cooked Majorcan tongue tends to be somewhat dull in colour. To combat this, most recipes include a thick sauce which is poured all over the sliced cooked meat. Then it is usually surrounded by puréed potatoes or vegetables before being sent to the table.

1 fresh calf's tongue, of about 1 kg (2¼ lb)	100 ml (3½ fl oz) dry white wine
1 medium onion, finely chopped	50 g (2 oz) blanched almonds
1 large, ripe tomato, peeled and chopped	1 tbsp roughly chopped parsley
1 whole head garlic	3 tbsp olive oil
2 bay leaves	salt
5 black peppercorns	500 g (1 lb) potatoes, cooked and puréed
1 clove	

Wash the tongue well under cold running water and leave it to soak in a bowl of cold water overnight. Next day, put it into a large saucepan, cover with cold water and bring to the boil. Boil for one minute only and then throw away the water.

Rinse the tongue well and then replace it in the clean saucepan, again covering it with cold water. Bring to the boil once more, but this time add some salt and simmer for 3 hours. Then remove the tongue, reserving the cooking liquid, and rinse it in cold water. Use a small sharp knife to peel the tongue, removing any small bones and pieces of fat and gristle.

Heat the oil in an earthenware casserole (a *greixonera*) and add the onion. When it is soft, but not coloured, add the tomato and simmer until a thick sauce has formed. Add the peeled garlic cloves, bay leaves, peppercorns, clove and white wine, and season to taste with salt. Leave to simmer slowly for 15 minutes, then add the tongue, cut into thick slices, and simmer for 15 minutes more.

Meanwhile, crush and pound the almonds in a mortar with the parsley, using a little of the tongue's cooking liquid to form a thick paste.

Remove the tongue from the sauce, arrange it on a hot serving dish and keep it warm. Pass the sauce through a sieve or vegetable mill. Mix a few tablespoons of it with the almond paste, then combine this with all the remaining sauce, heat through and pour over the tongue.

The sauce is of the consistency of bread sauce. If what you have made seems too thick, thin it with some of the remaining liquid in which the tongue was cooked.

Pipe the potato, or arrange it in spoonfuls, around the edge of the serving dish and serve at once. Serves 6 people.

TRIPES AMB SALSA

Callos con salsa   Majorcan tripe

English tripe has a stronger more pungent flavour than Majorcan tripe, due to a special dressing process and the two types do not interchange well as far as recipes are concerned.

All tripe in Majorca is sold untreated and must be properly prepared before cooking. Most butchers sell tripe in one piece, but if you buy it from the supermarkets, you will get a mixture of tripe, already cut into small pieces and prepacked, including cow-heel. It turns out well in the following recipe, but this tripe must also be treated first.

Instructions follow overleaf.

Wash the tripe well under running water and if it is in one piece, wring it out like a cloth. Then take a lemon, cut it in half and dip the cut ends in salt. Scrub the tripe hard with this. Then sprinkle it with vinegar and leave to soak in a little cold water for 15 minutes. Drain and put into a saucepan, cover with cold water, bring to the boil and simmer for 15 minutes. Drain under cold running water. The tripe is now blanched and ready for use, but will require a further 2 hours cooking before it is tender.

With the quantities given you will have enough for 4-6 people.

1 kg (2 ¼ lb) tripe	1 tbsp roughly chopped
100 g (3 ½ oz) fat bacon	parsley
1 medium onion, finely	1 bay leaf
chopped	30 g (1 oz) mild paprika
1 large ripe tomato,	100 g (3 ½ oz) *jamón*
skinned and chopped	*serrano* (ham)
1 slice fried bread	meat stock
4 garlic cloves	salt and pepper

Cut the cleaned and blanched tripe into bite sized pieces. Simmer for 2 hours in salted water.

In a frying-pan, fry the bacon, cut into dice, until the fat runs. Add the finely chopped onion and cook gently until transparent, then add the tomato. Cook until a thick sauce has formed.

With a pestle and mortar, crush the fried bread with the peeled garlic cloves and the parsley. Add the bay leaf and the paprika and pound together well.

Pour the the tomato and onion mixture into an earthenware casserole (a *greixonera*). Add the drained tripe and the *jamón serrano*, then stir in the garlic and breadcrumb mixture. Add enough meat stock to just cover the tripe and cook gently over a low flame for half an hour. The sauce should reduce and thicken slightly. Finally, season to taste.

This dish can also be made without the bacon or ham; instead add parboiled potatoes to the *greixonera* with the tripe.

Recipes for Beef

In Castilian Spanish, beef is *carne de vaca;* in Mallorquin, *carn de vaca.* Majorca's better restaurateurs, who cater for an international clientele, are well aware of the need to age meat to make it properly tender, and are able to serve succulent steaks and prime cuts from northern Spain, where the beef is excellent.

However, Majorca's own butchers have no tradition or experience of hanging meat. And their customers prefer beef which is bright red, showing that it was recently butchered. The result is that it is best to avoid buying steaks or cuts for roasting from Majorcan butchers. Their beef suffers most from not being hung, and what they offer should be reserved for stews or long, slow pot-roasting.

Unlike lamb and pork, cuts of beef do not correspond to English cuts and, to add to the confusion, there are several types and grades of beef on sale. However, both hypermarkets, Pryca and Continente, in Palma, prepack and label all their meat clearly which makes shopping, especially for beef, less fraught.

A Spanish dictionary will translate the word *ternera* as veal, but one glance at the bright red meat so labelled clearly shows that it is not. *Ternera* used to be a term for meat from one year old calves but this type of meat is now defined by the word *anojo* which specifically means a yearling. *Ternera* now loosely covers meat from young cattle over one year old; *ternera lechal* is veal — not commonly available but easily recognisable by its pale colour and high price. *Vacuna vieja* or *buey* is meat from mature cattle. Each type of cut beef is then graded: *primera* A or B, *segunda* or *tercera,* depending on which part of the animal the cut is taken from, though you will find that price is just as much an indication of quality as grading.

To simplify shopping at the local butcher's, who will not carry the range of clearly marked beef or graded cuts that the hypermarkets have, *carne de estofado* is stewing beef and will be sold either in one piece or cubed as you prefer; *redondo de ternera* is a cut of beef for pot roasting; and *carne picada* is minced meat. Some butchers, especially in the tourist areas, sell meat already minced, as do the hypermarkets, but there is a law which states that meat must be minced in front of the customer. Pre-minced meat can be inferior, so avoid it. When preparing your meat to be minced, the butcher will ask you if you want *ternera* — beef, *cerdo* — pork, or a mixture of the two — *una mezcla*.

Quite by accident a friend who had lived on the island for 30 years discovered an old Majorcan method of tenderizing very tough stewing beef. Her maid was preparing a stew and my friend happened to be in the kitchen as preparation started. She noticed that before doing anything else the cubed meat was dropped into a frying pan containing a small amount of water, brought to the boil and, over a medium heat and with occasional turning, allowed to absorb all the water. The meat — a grey colour — was then fried in the normal manner for making stews. The maid, on being asked about it, expressed surprise that the *señora* did not know of this way of softening beef — 'everybody does it'. Her proportions were about 125 ml (4½ fl oz) of water to 1 kilo (2¼ lb) of meat, but this is not an inflexible formula and, if the amount of liquid turns out to be too much, one simply pours some away.

I have used this method with great success many times since hearing about it. Previously I had to cook some stewing meat for 3 to 4 hours before it was tender. With this method it is tender in 1½-2 hours.

CARN A LA 'MADÒ MARIA'

Carne a la 'Madò Maria'   Madò Maria's stew

800 g (1¾ lb) stewing   16 toasted hazelnuts or
  beef (*carne de estofado*)   almonds
  cut into pieces   4 garlic cloves
80 g (3 oz) lard or the   1 tbsp roughly chopped
  equivalent in olive oil   parsley
1 onion, finely chopped   ½ litre (18 fl oz) meat
½ tbsp mild paprika   stock or water
2 cloves   1 bay leaf
4 whole black   salt
  peppercorns

Place the pieces of beef in a frying-pan with slightly less than
125 ml (4½ fl oz) of water, and set it over a high heat. Turn the
meat occasionally as the water comes to the boil and is absorbed.

Next, heat the lard or oil in a casserole and brown the meat
all over. Add the onion and leave it to fry on the lowest possible *slow-*
heat. Meanwhile grind together the paprika, cloves and *cooker.*
peppercorns and add this mixture to the meat in the casserole.

Pound the hazelnuts (or almonds) with the peeled garlic cloves
and parsley, adding a little of the stock until a thick paste has
formed. Combine this with the rest of the stock and pour it over
the meat. Add the bay leaf and season with salt.

Cover and simmer slowly for 1½ hours or until the meat is
tender.

CARN DE SANT FRANCESC

Carne de San Francisco   St Francis' beef

800 g (1 ¾ lb) stewing beef
  (*carne de estofado*) in one
  piece
1 tbsp lard or olive oil
1 large onion, finely
  chopped
1 large red pepper, diced

400 g (14 oz) ripe
  tomatoes, peeled and
  chopped
1 bay leaf
1 tbsp chopped parsley
salt and pepper

Cut the meat into thick slices and follow the tenderizing method as described in the previous recipe.

Heat the lard or oil in a casserole and lightly fry the onion, pepper and tomatoes until the tomatoes have formed a purée. Add the slices of meat, bay leaf, parsley and a little water. Cover and simmer slowly for 1 ½ hours, or until the meat is tender. Remove the meat from the casserole to a warm serving dish.

Pass the sauce through a sieve or vegetable mill. Pour it over the meat and serve surrounded with sauté potatoes.

AUFEGAT

Espinilla de buey rehogada   Spiced shin of beef

'*Olla podria, el coch instruit en fer aguits, pastes i confitures.*' Written in the third quarter of the 18th century by the Augustine monk Fray Jaime Marti de Mallorca (d 1785)*, the document with this title was an exuberant manuscript in the Baroque style, where fruits, tomatoes, bell peppers, and other novel foods from the New World were fully integrated into the recipes. In it, as Dr Rudolf Grewe has pointed out, appeared a new culinary technique, the *aufegat* (which literally means 'suffocated'), where a dish is cooked in very little liquid, in a casserole which is covered by setting another casserole (full of water, to weigh it down in a tight fit) on top of it.

Altogether, it seems that this Majorcan was a highly original writer, whose work deserves more attention.

As a step in the right direction, Luis Ripoll, in his *Cocina de las Balearas,* has printed the text of the original *aufegat* recipe:

> Take a piece of shin of beef and lard it. Arrange it in a casserole with lard, *sobrasada,* onion and a whole head of garlic, vinegar, marjoram, tomato and bay leaf. All this is placed on top of the meat once it has been browned. Now cover the casserole with a dish containing water after adding just a small quantity of stock sufficient only to cook the meat as well as the spices.

The following is my own interpretation of this recipe (I have substituted kitchen foil for the casserole full of water to achieve the right fit).

800 g-1 kg (1 ¾-2 ¼ lb)
  shin of beef (*espinilla de buey*) in one piece
25 g (1 oz) lard
25 g (1 oz) *sobrasada,* cut into pieces
1 whole head garlic
2 tsp dried marjoram

1 heaped tsp paprika
1 small piece cinnamon
6 black peppercorns
2 cloves
1 tbsp vinegar
¼ litre (9 fl oz) good meat stock

Brown the piece of meat in the lard in a casserole. Add the *sobrasada,* the peeled but whole garlic cloves, the marjoram and paprika; plus the cinnamon, peppercorns and cloves ground together. Pour in the vinegar and the meat stock, which should come to no more than half way up the side of the meat. Cover the casserole with foil and then put on the lid and cook on the lowest flame for 2 ½ hours.

Serve hot, sliced, with the sauce — which should have reduced to a thick, spicy red consistency.

*As this book is going to press, I have found out that Fray Jaime Marti's manuscript has been edited by Joan Miralles and Francesca Cantallops and published under the title *Receptari de cuina del segle XVIII* by Universitat de les Illes Balears/ Publicacions de l'Abadia de Montserrat, 1989.

ESTOFAT DE BOU

Estofado de buey   Beef casserole

It is interesting to note that Coloma Abrinas Vidal in *Cocina Selecta Mallorquina* gives her own version of *aufegat*, obviously originating from the same 18th century source. I have made only slight changes. She would have used twice as many onions and would have added fried potatoes 10 minutes before the end of cooking, whereas I prefer to serve them separately so that they do not become soggy. Also I have used kitchen foil to achieve a tight seal on the earthenware casserole more easily and effectively than by the technique of covering it with a similar casserole full of water.

800 g-1 kg (1¾-2¼ lb) stewing beef (*carne de buey*), in thick slices
80 g (3 oz) lard
2 onions, roughly sliced
2 large ripe tomatoes, chopped

1 whole head garlic, the cloves peeled but whole
100 ml (3½ fl oz) dry white wine
1 bay leaf
4 peppercorns
salt

Place all the ingredients together, without any previous cooking, in a lidded casserole; and cover it first with a layer of kitchen foil and then with the lid. Place it over a very low flame on top of the stove and leave it to cook slowly for several hours, at least 2½. Remember to shake the pan occasionally, but do not remove the lid.

The meat will be very tender and the other ingredients will have disintegrated to form a thick sauce.

Pork Recipes

In the section on important ingredients (pp 32-6) I have described the pork products which feature regularly in Majorcan cookery. The quality of the pork on the island is excellent. It is the most popular meat in Majorca, along with chicken; the two account for some 80% of the meat eaten. Pork is *porc* in Mallorquin, but *cerdo* in Castilian.

Lomo de cerdo or pork loin is probably the best value for money — lean with no waste. It is sold sliced into steaks for simple frying, but in a single piece for roasting or pot-roasting. Loin of pork and pork chops benefit from spending a few hours in a marinade of lemon juice, olive oil and seasoning before cooking.

Carne magra is pork cut from the leg and is used for stewing (either in one piece or cubed) or for mince; legs of pork for roasting cut in the English fashion are rare.

LLOM AMB ESCLATA-SANGS

Lomo con setas   Loin of pork with wild mushrooms

A dish for late autumn and early winter when the *setas* (wild mushrooms) are in season.

Marinate slices of pork loin with salt, black pepper, lemon juice and olive oil for an hour or so. Remove the stems from wild mushrooms and place a small piece of skinned *sobrasada* in each cap. Place the caps in an ovenproof dish, and sprinkle them with salt, pepper and a little lemon juice. Put a tiny piece of lard on each or pour over some olive oil. Bake them for 10-15 minutes in a hot oven.

Meanwhile fry the slices of pork loin in olive oil until cooked and golden on both sides. Put them on a warm serving dish with the cooked mushrooms, pouring the juice from the mushrooms into the frying-pan. For garnish, you can then fry slices of bread in the same pan.

185

LLOM AMB ESCLATA-SANGS I SALSA

Lomo con setas y salsa	Pork loin and wild mushrooms with a sauce

1½ kg (3¼ lb) loin of pork, in one piece
½ kg (1 lb) onions
3 tbsp olive oil
¼ kg (9 oz) tomatoes, skinned and seeded
¼ litre (9 fl oz) meat stock

100 ml (3½ fl oz) dry white wine
1 kg (2¼ lb) *setas*
½ litre (18 fl oz) bechamel sauce (recipe on p 78)
salt and pepper

Season the piece of pork and wrap in baking foil. Roast in a hot oven at 200°C (390°F, gas mark 5) for one hour.

Slice the onions very thinly in rounds and, in a large saucepan, soften in the hot oil. Add the tomatoes, meat stock and white wine and leave to simmer until a thick sauce has formed. Blend the sauce in a blender, pass it through a sieve, return it to the cleaned pan, and season it.

Clean and cut the *setas* into thin strips and add to the tomato sauce. Simmer for 5 minutes.

Heat the bechamel sauce and pour it into an earthenware casserole (a *greixonera*). Slice the pork, add the slices to the bechamel sauce, then cover the whole lot with the tomato and mushroom sauce. Place in a very hot oven for 10 minutes, then serve at once.

LLOM DE PORC AMB COL

Lomo con col   Pork with cabbage

8 large green cabbage
  leaves, whole
a few more cabbage
  leaves, shredded
8 slices pork loin (*lomo de
  cerdo*)
olive oil
8 slices *sobrasada*
8 slices *butifarron*

1 medium onion, finely
  chopped
400 g (14 oz) ripe tomatoes,
  skinned and chopped
3 garlic cloves, finely
  chopped
¼ tbsp mild paprika
salt and pepper
1 tbsp pine nuts
1 tbsp raisins

Blanch the large cabbage leaves, with the stems neatly removed, in salted water for 4 minutes. Drain and spread each leaf on top of a work surface.

Fry the slices of pork loin on both sides in olive oil; place a slice on top of each cabbage leaf and top with a slice of *sobrasada* and *butifarron*. Season and wrap up the meat with the leaf like a parcel.

In the same frying-pan, adding more oil if necessary, soften the onion; add the tomato, garlic and paprika and cook until thickened. Season with salt and pepper and add the pine nuts and raisins.

Place the cabbage parcels in an ovenproof casserole on top of the shredded cabbage leaves and pour over the sauce. The sauce should not quite cover the cabbage parcels; if necessary, add a little water. Cover the casserole and simmer slowly on top of the stove for 1-1½ hours.

PORCELLA AL FORN

Lechona al horno   Roast suckling pig

Departing from a small lunch party given by a local
restaurateur, where a roast suckling pig weighing about 3 kg
(6¾ lb) had been served, my Majorcan companions remarked
that the best suckling pig weighed about 12 kg (25 lb) and should
ideally be roasted in a wood-fired oven or over an open wood fire.

It is illegal in England to sell the very small suckling pigs that
are so easily bought in Majorca, and perhaps just as well, for
these tiny piglets, although ideal for small family meals and
ovens, lack flavour and meat content. Besides which, it seems a
shame to kill them so young.

However, few modern ovens will take a larger animal and,
although many bakers in villages and in Palma still use the old
wood-burning oven and happily accept trays of suckling pigs for
roasting, it is a feat of organisation beyond the powers of a casual
visitor. The best way around the problem is to buy half a suckling
pig or even a quarter of one — butchers will cut them up. Then,
although you cannot have quite such an attractive display, you
will at least be eating the best meat.

Suckling pigs, as well as turkeys, are still the main Christmas
dish. In the past, rough enclosures would have been set up at
various points around Palma two days before Christmas. Here,
under a sign announcing *'se matan lechonas'*, the little pigs would
be slaughtered, soused with boiling water which was kept
bubbling in a cauldron over a fire, scraped and quickly made
ready for cooking. Nowadays, *lechona* is easily available, ready
for cooking, from all the butchers' shops, especially at weekends
and for *fiestas*. It is also a standard restaurant dish and well worth
trying, for the portions are more likely to be cut from a large
suckling pig than a small one.

The following method of roasting a suckling pig is for an
electric or butane gas oven.

a suckling pig weighing   ¼ litre (9 fl oz) olive oil
  2½-3 kg (around 6 lb)   plenty of salt
4 large lemons

Wash and dry the meat thoroughly. Then rub it all over with plenty of salt, squeeze on the juice of all the lemons, pour over the olive oil, and leave it to marinate overnight in the refrigerator.

Preheat the oven to its hottest point. Place the pig in a large oiled roasting pan. If, as assumed here, you have succumbed to the attraction of a small piglet, it must be placed down with is legs splayed out. (If, on the other hand, you have bought half a larger suckling pig, it will have been sliced in half through the head, and you place the cut side down). Pour the marinade juices over the pig, place the pan in the centre of the oven, and turn the oven heat down low. Cook slowly for 2 hours, then turn the heat up very high for about 45 minutes, basting frequently. When the skin is crisp and deep reddish gold it is ready to serve.

In the last part of the cooking process, take care that the pig does not burn; cover ears and snout with foil and be prepared to adjust the temperature now and again.

Do not attempt to carve thin slices; instead, cut thick chunks, pour over the cooking juices and serve with tiny roast potatoes.

COSTELLETES DE PORCELLA

Costillas de lechona   Rib chops from suckling pig

Rib chops from large suckling pigs are an excellent buy for a simple, easily prepared meal and are available from most butchers' shops.

Marinate the chops in plenty of lemon juice, salt and pepper for an hour or two. Heat some olive oil in a frying-pan and fry the chops with several large, unpeeled garlic cloves until crisp and golden on both sides. Serve with the pan juices poured over and garnish with slices of lemon.

FETGE DE PORC AMB CEBA

Higado de cerdo encebollado   Liver and onions

This is a dish for spring when the wild fennel is just sprouting.

400 g (14 oz) pigs' liver
75 ml (2½ fl oz) olive
  oil
400 g (14 oz) onions,
  thinly sliced

2 garlic cloves, peeled and
  chopped
1 tbsp finely chopped fresh
  fennel leaves
salt and pepper

Wash the liver, dry it and cut it into slices. Heat the oil in a frying-pan and brown the liver quickly over a high flame, then remove from the pan, season, and reserve on a plate.

Fry the onion in the same oil until it is golden. Then add the garlic and the liver, together with the juice that has collected on the plate. Cover the frying-pan and leave to cook on a very low heat for 10 minutes. Finally, sprinkle on the fennel, adjust the seasoning if necessary, and cook for a further 5 minutes.

RONYONS AMB SALSA

Riñones con salsa   Pork kidneys in a tomato sauce

The sauce can be made in advance and the kidneys finished off at the last moment. A recipe for 4-6 people.

800 g (1¾ lb) pigs'
  kidneys
4 tbsp olive oil
1 onion, finely chopped
3 large ripe tomatoes,
  skinned and chopped

1 tbsp finely chopped
  parsley
100 ml (3½ fl oz) white
  wine
salt
ground white pepper

Clean the kidneys, cut them into small, very thin slices and reserve.

In a frying pan, heat the olive oil and gently fry the onion until soft. Add the tomatoes and parsley and simmer for 10 minutes. Pour in the white wine, season with salt and white pepper and simmer for a further 10 minutes.

When you are ready to serve, and not before, stir the kidneys into the hot sauce, cook for 2 minutes only and serve at once. The kidneys will be very tender.

PUES DE PORC

Pies de cerdo   Pigs' trotters

4 pigs' trotters, split in
   half
1 large onion, finely
   chopped
50 g (2 oz) lard or 2 tbsp
   olive oil
1 large ripe tomato, peeled
   and chopped
30 g (1 oz) mild paprika
3 slices white bread (cut
   from a *barra grande,* a
   French-style loaf)

4 large garlic cloves
4 black peppercorns
1 bay leaf
1 tbsp roughly chopped
   parsley
1 tsp salt
2 eggs
flour
oil for frying

Place the trotters in a saucepan of cold water and bring to the boil. Continue to boil for 10 minutes, then drain, and rinse the trotters well under running water. Singe off any hairs if necessary, rinse again and replace in the cleaned saucepan. Cover with cold water, bring to the boil and then simmer gently, covered, for 2 hours.

Soften the onion in the lard or oil, then add the tomato and simmer until it has formed a thick sauce. Stir in the paprika and ½ litre (18 fl oz) of the trotters' cooking liquid and leave to simmer slowly.

Meanwhile, fry the slices of bread until golden on both sides and then crush them in a mortar with the garlic cloves, peppercorns, bay leaf, parsley and salt. Stir this mixture into the tomato sauce and let it simmer gently for a few minutes.

Cut the halved pigs' trotters in half again, dip them in the beaten egg, then coat them in flour. Fry in hot oil until golden all over and serve at once with the sauce.

Lamb Recipes

Spanish lamb (*cordero,* but *anyell* in Mallorquin) is eaten at a much younger age than in Britain but the cuts of meat, though smaller, are similar to English cuts. It is well-flavoured and of high quality; but may be tough through lack of proper hanging. If so, I find that marinating the meat for just a few hours in a little lemon juice, olive oil, salt and pepper is all that is required, although a leg of lamb or steaks cut from the leg are better marinated overnight.

Lamb is the traditional meat for Easter. At one time, Lent was strictly observed and, during its six weeks' duration, Palma butchers were forbidden to sell meat to anyone other than invalids, and signs forbidding the sale of meat were hung in all butchers' shops. On Good Friday, the last day of Lent, the butchers publicly burnt these signs and in the afternoon went from street to street offering to slaughter lambs which would have been purchased by the *Palmesanos* a few days earlier at a fair held outside the city walls. Then each household would make the traditional Easter lamb pies (*panades*).

Strict rules existed for meals taken on Easter Sunday. It was usual to fast from noon on Saturday until after the Easter morning Mass and procession and then to eat a huge breakfast which includes *frit,* a dish made from the liver, heart and lungs of the slaughtered lamb. A substantial lunch was served in mid-afternoon, including a stew made with the lamb left over from making *panades.* Thus, all the lamb slaughtered on Good Friday afternoon would have been used up — even the skins, for tanners followed the butchers, offering to buy them up.

Of these traditions, only the making of *panades* (for which there is a recipe on p 88) and the reluctance to hang meat have survived.

ESPATLA D'ANYELL ASSAONADA

Paletilla de cordero en adobo   Marinated shoulder of lamb

When Majorcans cook shoulders or legs of lamb, they usually make four or five deep cuts in them, just deep enough to split the bone. This is because they prefer their meat on the bone. Once the joint is cooked, the meat is served in chunks rather than in slices. A leg of lamb can be substituted for shoulder in this recipe.

1 shoulder of lamb weighing 1-1¼ kg (2¼-3 lb)	2 tbsp flour
a few sprigs of parsley	salt and pepper
1 large bay leaf	2 tbsp olive oil
2 large onions, sliced	100 g (3½ oz) belly pork (*panceta*) sliced
2 large carrots, sliced	¼ litre (9 fl oz) meat stock
5 black peppercorns	1 tsp dried thyme
100 ml (3½ fl oz) dry white wine	

garlic
herbas beunas - mint,

Make sure that the butcher makes four or five deep cuts in the shoulder. Place the shoulder in a dish and arrange the sprigs of parsley on top, together with the bay leaf, sliced onions and carrots. Season, and pour over the white wine. Leave to marinate overnight.

Remove the meat and pat it dry with kitchen paper. Strain and reserve the marinade. Coat the shoulder with the flour, season with salt and pepper. Heat the olive oil in a flat earthenware dish or a roasting-pan and fry the slices of belly pork until golden, then add the lamb and fry it on both sides until it too is golden. Pour the marinade and the meat stock over all this and sprinkle on the thyme. Roast at 180°C (355°F, gas mark 4) for one hour.

When the joint is done, just slice through the cuts made by the butcher and serve the meat in thick chunks — with roast potatoes and the roasting-pan juices, which will have thickened to make a delicious gravy.

This dish serves 2 people.

GREIXERA DE CARN *Lamb casserole*.

'Greixera' de carne   Meat casserole

This dish is certainly of Moorish origin. It was originally made with lamb in the spring and mutton in the autumn; but nowadays, in the absence of mutton, it is strictly a lamb (or, occasionally, beef) dish, with the fruits and vegetables added according to seasonal availability.

800 g (1¾ lb) stewing lamb, cut into cubes
1 tbsp lard or olive oil
1 large onion, finely chopped
1 large ripe tomato, peeled and chopped
100 g (3 oz) fresh *tocino* or pork fat, diced
100 g (3 oz) *butifarra* or *camaiot,* sliced
100 g (3 oz) *longaniza,* sliced

vegetables according to the season; diced potato/carrots/green peppers, beans, peas, sliced artichokes ...
fresh fruit ditto: halved green plums, apricots or cherries, grapes, sliced sour peaches, apples ...
fresh or dried oregano
salt and pepper
ground cinnamon

Heat the lard in a frying-pan and gently fry the cubes of lamb a few at a time until brown all over. Remove them with a slotted spoon and reserve them. In the same fat, fry the onion until soft, then add the tomato and fry gently until a thick sauce has formed.

In an earthenware casserole (a *greixonera*), arrange the fried meat, the *tocino* and the *butifarra* or *camaiot* in layers, with the prepared fruit and vegetables and the onion and tomato mixture separating each meat layer. Season each layer of meat well as you put it in. Add some finely chopped fresh oregano to the various layers; or some dried oregano, used sparingly.

Pour cold water into the *greixonera* so that it comes about half way up the side, bring to the boil on top of the stove and then bake at 190°C (370°F, gas mark 5) for 1-1½ hours. Before serving, sprinkle with ground cinnamon.

GUISAT D'ANYELL AMB ALBERGÍNIES

Guisado de cordero
con berenjenas

Ragout of lamb with
aubergines

For this recipe I am indebted to *Cocina Balear* by Anna Maria Calera. This is a dish of obvious Middle Eastern origin; a very similar recipe appears in Claudia Roden's *Middle Eastern Cookery:* 'meat stew with aubergines'.

1 kg (2¼ lb) breast of
    lamb, cut into pieces
150 g (5 oz) lard, or 175 ml
    (5 fl oz) olive oil
2 onions, finely sliced
4 garlic cloves, finely
    chopped
½ tbsp flour
200 ml (7 fl oz) dry
    white wine

½ kg (1 lb) tomatoes
    peeled and chopped
1 bay leaf
½ tsp dried oregano
½ tsp dried thyme
ground nutmeg
ground white pepper
salt
4 aubergines
about ¼ litre (9 fl oz)
    oil for frying

Heat the lard or oil in a frying pan and fry the lamb a few pieces at a time. Brown the pieces all over and, using a slotted spoon, put them in a casserole. Then fry the onions in the same fat until they just start to take colour. Add the onions to the meat in the casserole and set over a low heat. Stir in the garlic and the flour, then add the tomatoes and the white wine. Season with salt, white pepper and plenty of ground nutmeg, and add the bay leaf, oregano and thyme. If you think there is not enough liquid in the casserole, top it up with a little water. Cover and simmer for 1½-2 hours.

Meanwhile, peel and dice the aubergines, place them in a colander and sprinkle them liberally with salt. Put a heavy plate on top. Leave them for at least an hour to allow the bitter juices to seep out; then rinse them in cold running water and pat dry with kitchen paper. Dust them with flour and fry them in hot oil until golden, then drain them, and add to the casserole 10 minutes before serving.

FRIT MALLORQUI

Frito mallorquin   Majorcan lamb fry

Although the Majorcans say that the best *frito mallorquin* is made with Easter lamb, the dish is so popular in Majorca that it is available all year round in *tapas* bars, in restaurants (as either a first or second course), and in the home. It is made with the heart, liver and lungs — collectively known as an *asadura* — of lamb. A similar dish, known as *frito de matanzas* is made with pork *asadura*. Both hypermarkets, Pryca and Continente, are good places to buy lamb *asadura*. It is prepacked and clearly labelled, which saves the non-Spanish speaker from getting into a muddle with the local butcher who will not always have an *asadura* available.

1 *asadura de cordero* (see above) weighing about 1 kg (2 ¼ lb)
¼ litre (9 fl oz) olive oil
½ kg (1 lb 2 oz) potatoes
250 g (9 oz) onions, finely sliced
1 large red pepper (optional), diced

5 large spring onions, roughly chopped including the green parts
2 bay leaves
8 cloves garlic
1 tsp mild paprika
plenty of fresh fennel
1 small piece dried red chilli pepper
salt and pepper

Dice the heart, liver and lungs fairly small. Peel the potatoes and cut them into chips — of whatever size suits you, there is no standard size. Fry the chips in the olive oil, preferably in a *greixonera*, until soft, then remove them with a slotted spoon and reserve them.

Fry the diced *asadura* in the remaining oil until lightly coloured. Add the onion and the red pepper. Leave over a low heat to soften the vegetables for about 10 minutes, then add the spring onions, bay leaves, garlic cloves (whole and unpeeled), and paprika, plus the chopped fennel (which, in spring, would be the green frond-like leaves and at other times the dried fennel flower head and stems), and the chilli pepper. Season, and cook gently on a medium heat for 10 minutes, stirring occasionally.

Add the potatoes, mixing them in well, heat through and serve at once.

This is a dish that can be made in advance and reheated, even after the chipped potatoes have been added, but it is best eaten the day it is made.

CERVELLES D'ANYELL AMB SALSA DE CHAMPIGNONS

Sesos de cordero con salsa
de champiñones

Lambs' brains with mushroom sauce

4 lambs' brains
4 rashers of bacon
25 g (1 oz) lard
1 small onion, finely
  chopped
200 g (7 oz) mushrooms,
  finely sliced

½ tsp dried savory
½ tsp dried oregano
salt and pepper
½ tbsp lightly toasted
  flour
¼ litre (9 fl oz) good
  meat stock

Carefully rinse the brains under cold running water. If necessary, remove any fine membrane covering them, though lambs' brains are now specially prepared and prepacked in Spain and the membrane is generally removed. Soak the brains in salted water for an hour or so and then gently rinse again.

Place the brains in a saucepan, cover them with cold water, bring to the boil and simmer for 5 minutes. Drain them, dry them on kitchen paper, then wrap each brain in a slice of bacon and secure it with a toothpick. Melt the lard in a frying-pan and fry the brains on a medium to high flame until golden. Remove and keep warm.

Fry the onion in the same fat as the brains until golden, then add the mushrooms, savory and oregano together with salt and pepper. Stir in the toasted flour and the meat stock. Simmer gently for 10 minutes, stirring frequently, until the sauce is thick. Add the fried brains, and simmer just long enough to heat everything through before serving.

197

Desserts

Sweet dishes (*plats dolsos* in Mallorquin, *postres,* meaning 'afters', in Castilian) are not important in Majorcan cookery. Most ordinary meals end with fruit of the season; always available and good. A special family gathering or *fiesta* would finish with cakes bought from the local baker or cake shop. In restaurants puddings are usually bought in, chilled or frozen and heavily sweetened.

Yet Majorca does have a tradition of well-made sweet dishes, for it is here that the culinary influence of the Moors is still strongly felt. The various jams, cakes, pastries and iced sweet drinks which can be traced back to them represent the strength of Majorcan sweet cookery.

The snag is the lack of any major dairy production, which has meant that pork lard is used in pastries rather than butter, still an expensive luxury.

Occasionally various egg custards, fritters or cakes are made at home, especially at Christmas, but some pastries are so well made by the bakers and specialist cake shops that it seems pointless to try to reproduce them at home. A good example is the *ensaimada,* a sweet, airy yeast bun. The name comes from *saim,* Mallorquin for the lard of highest quality which is a main ingredient. This bun is one of Majorca's most famous products and is not made anywhere else in Spain. It is said to have originated with the Moors, for its coiled shape resembles a Moorish turban. It comes in one standard size, plain with just a sprinkling of icing sugar, popular with morning coffee; and in various sizes filled with cream, confectioner's custard or angel's hair jam. Large filled ones are sold by all bakers on Sundays and *fiestas.*

During Lent, *ensaimadas* studded with pieces of *sobrasada* and pork fat were made; an acquired taste, but addictive. These *ensaimadas* are now quite commonly available.

Although I favour buying *ensaimadas,* and have never

attempted to make one, I give this recipe from Lourdes March's
La Cocina Mediterranea for those who would like to try. Señora
March is renowned for her clear and precise instructions; if
anyone can show the way she can.

ENSAIMADA

Ensaimada   Majorcan yeast bun

1 kg (2 ¼ lb) strong white   6 egg yolks
   flour   350 g (12 oz) sugar
275 ml (10 fl oz) water   400 g (14 oz) finest lard
80 g (nearly 3 oz) fresh   100 ml (3 ½ fl oz) olive oil
   yeast

Put the yeast in a small bowl and mix it with 3 teaspoons of the
water and 1 teaspoon of the flour. Cover with a clean dry cloth.
When the mixture has risen, put it into a larger bowl and add the
rest of the water (at blood temperature). Next, add the egg yolks,
the sugar, and a teaspoon of the lard. Mix all this thoroughly,
then add the rest of the flour, little by little, to make your dough.

Work the dough by dividing it into small pieces and massing
it all together again. Repeat this operation several times. Then
form the dough into a ball, cover it with a clean cloth and leave
it to rise. When it has doubled in size, add the olive oil by
kneading it in slowly. After this, leave it to rest for 2 hours.

Knead the dough and then roll it out with a rolling pin on a
marble top. Spread the remaining lard over it, roll it up, and
then roll it out again — very thin, like paper.

Next, roll up the dough again to make a long cylinder of it. Lay
this out on a large greased baking tray in a spiral, starting from
the centre and working out. Leave it for 12 hours in a warm
place, covered with a clean cloth.

Then bake it in a medium oven (200°C/390°F/gas mark 5)
until it is coloured golden. Remove it and sprinkle it with icing
sugar.

BUNYOLS

Buñuelos   Doughnuts

Buñuelos are certainly of Arabic origin as, under various names, these light fritters appear in the cookery of many Middle Eastern countries. They are popular throughout Spain, each region having its own particular recipes. In Majorca *buñuelos* are traditonally eaten on the eve of the Feast of the Virgins, 20 October and on the feast day itself, 21 October, though the customs accompanying this tradition have now died out. On the eve of the feast, young unmarried men used to go round the village, serenading outside the houses of young unmarried girls. The girls' mothers would offer them drinks and *buñuelos,* but the girls themselves would be kept firmly out of sight. Any favoured young men would be invited back to the house the next day.

    Buñuelos are also prepared for the Feast of All Saints on 1 November, the day Spaniards visit the cemeteries, laying flowers on family graves, often having a picnic, and leaving everything tidy and colourful for the Feast of All Souls on the next day. Bakeries sell *buñuelos* on both days.

BUNYOLS DE VENT

Buñuelos de viento   Light airy doughnuts

In a saucepan heat together 100 ml (3 ½ fl oz) of water and 100 ml (3 ½ fl oz) of milk with a small nut of lard. When the liquid has boiled, remove from the heat and stir in enough strong, sifted flour to make a stiff paste. Leave to cool, then add, one by one, 3 eggs, beating each in well.

    Using a teaspoon, take spoonfuls of the batter and deep fry them in olive oil (not too hot). Add only a few at a time and fry gently. They will puff up quickly and rise to the surface. Gently turn them over and fry until they are golden brown all over. Remove with a slotted spoon, drain, and serve at once, sprinkled with sugar and cinnamon. They will be light and airy and hollow inside.

BUNYOLS DE PATATA

Buñuelos de patata   *Potato doughnuts*

200 g (7 oz) potatoes
100 g (3 oz) sugar
2 egg yolks

for the batter
2 tbsp flour
1 egg
½ tbsp olive oil
1 tbsp sweet dessert wine
2 egg whites

Either bake the potatoes in their jackets, then peel and mash them, or carefully boil them, peeled, and mash, but the aim is to obtain as dry a mixture as possible.

In a saucepan over a low heat combine the mashed potato and sugar. Beat together until the sugar has dissolved. When the mixture is very hot, remove from the heat and at once add the two beaten egg yolks. Beat with a fork until the mixture thickens. Pour onto a large dinner plate and leave to cool completely.

To make the batter, sift the flour into a bowl and start to beat in the egg. Beat well and add, as you beat, the olive oil and sweet wine. If necessary, add a very small amount of water, but the batter should be thick and creamy. Whisk the two egg whites until they stand in peaks and fold into the batter.

Make walnut-sized balls with the cold potato mixture. If it is not stiff enough to form into balls, add a small amount of flour, but just shaping the balls with well-floured hands may be sufficient. Dip the balls into the batter and drop at once into a pan of not-too-hot olive oil. Fry a few at a time. They will quickly rise to the surface in puffed up round shapes. Turn over with a slotted spoon and remove when crisp and golden on both sides. Remove with the slotted spoon and drain on kitchen paper. While they are still hot, dip them into clear honey and lift out again. Serve hot or cold dusted with ground cinnamon.

COQUES DE PATATAS

Coca de patatas   Potato buns

A sweet, light, airy yeast bun that is good with morning coffee, but is not as common as the *ensaimada*. Ordinary potatoes can be substituted for sweet potatoes which are only in season from late September to March. This recipe makes about 16 rolls.

500 g (1 lb) strong flour (warmed)	100-150 g (3½-5 oz) sugar
400 g (14 oz) sweet potatoes	75 g (2 oz) lard
3 eggs	15 g (½ oz) fresh yeast (about the size of a walnut)
about ¼ litre (9 fl oz) milk	

It is difficult to give an exact liquid measure; you may have to add more milk after the yeast is mixed in with the flour, or be prepared to add just a little more flour.

Cook the potatoes by peeling and boiling until soft and mashing them, keeping the mixture as dry as possible. (Better still, bake them in the oven in their jackets, then remove the pulp and mash it well. This latter method gives a drier mixture).

Slightly warm half the milk. Cream the yeast with one teaspoon of sugar and stir it into the warm milk. Leave for 10 to 15 minutes or until the mixture has frothed up. Rub the lard into the warmed flour, stir in the sweet potato mixture together with the beaten egg and sugar, and add the milk and yeast mixture. Knead, adding the rest of the milk (warmed) if required, until the mixture comes away from the sides of the bowl cleanly. Let it rise in a warm spot for half an hour. Knock the dough down and knead again.

Shape the dough into large circular rolls and place on a greased baking tray. Prove for 20-25 minutes; the rolls will have doubled in size. Bake until golden brown in a medium oven (200°C/390°F/gas mark 5) for about 15 minutes.

LLESQUES DE PA

Rabanadas de pan   Slices of bread

A way of using up stale *coca de patatas*. Cut it into slices and moisten them in milk. Dip the slices in beaten egg and fry them on both sides until golden in hot olive oil. Serve sprinkled with ground sugar and cinnamon.

MENJAR BLANC

Manjar blanco   Blancmange

A dish of Moorish origin, very close to the Arab dish *Muhallabia* described in Claudia Roden's *A Book of Middle Eastern Food*. Historically minded readers may like to know that in a recent essay in the Prospect Books journal *PPC* (number 31) Charles Perry, the distinguished historian of Arab food, explores its history and concludes surprisingly that almonds were not, originally, an essential ingredient.

This used to be very popular served at street *fiestas* in Palma but is now something of a rarity.

1 litre (36 fl oz) milk	100 g (3½ oz) finely
65 g (2 oz) sugar	ground almonds
33 g (1 oz) cornflour	peel of 1 lemon
85 g (2½ oz) rice flour	small stick of cinnamon

Mix the rice flour and cornflour together in a bowl and dissolve with some of the milk. Put the rest of the milk in a saucepan with the sugar, lemon peel and cinnamon stick and over a very low heat bring it to blood heat. Now stir in the rice and cornflour mixture together with the ground almonds. Stir continuously over the low heat until the mixture has thickened sufficiently to coat the back of a spoon. Cook carefully for a few more minutes and remove from the heat. Cool slightly and then remove the lemon peel and cinnamon stick. Pour into individual glasses and chill.

Serve sprinkled with ground cinnamon and chopped almonds.

PUDIN

Pudin   Majorcan pudding

A very popular Majorcan dish. In restaurants it is one of the few sweet dishes always made on the premises; and there are many variations. This recipe is adapted for home use from the one used in the restaurant Ca'n Joan in Genova.

2 tbsp sugar	5 eggs
½ tsp ground cinnamon	2-3 stale *ensaimadas* or
¾ litre (27 fl oz) milk	*cocas de patatas*
peel of ½ lemon	4 tbsp sugar for
	caramelising

Mix together the 2 tablespoons of sugar and the cinnamon with a little milk to form a paste. Heat ½ litre (18 fl oz) of the milk very slowly with the lemon peel. When it is hot, but not boiling, pour it over the sugar and cinnamon and stir until the sugar is melted. Add the rest of the milk, remove the lemon peel and beat in the eggs.

Put the 4 tablespoons of sugar for caramelising into a saucepan and heat it, dry, over a moderate heat, stirring all the time with a wooden spoon. It will melt quickly, turning golden, then brown. As soon as it turns brown, remove it from the heat and stir in 2 tablespoons of water, taking care as the sugar will bubble up quickly. Stir over a low heat until it becomes a smooth syrup.

Pour this syrup into a 1 litre loaf-style tin. Fill the tin with broken pieces of *ensaimadas* or *cocas de patata* and then pour the egg and milk mixture on top. Stand the tin in a roasting tray filled with water and bake at 180°C (355°F, gas mark 4) for one hour, adding more water to the tray as it evaporates. The pudding should be slightly risen and the top a deep golden brown. Cool in the tin and then turn out onto a serving dish. Serve cold, cut into slices.

BUNYOLS DE POMES

Fritos de puré de manzana   Apple fritters

3 large apples; of those
   available in Majorca,
   Starking are probably
   best
3 tbsp flour

1 ½ tbsp sugar
sugar for coating
olive oil for frying, about
   ¾ litre (27 fl oz)

Peel and grate the apples and mix with the flour and the sugar.
Divide into small portions and drop them, a few at a time, into
the hot oil with a spoon. As the fritters rise to the surface, turn
them over to cook evenly and when they are a golden colour all
over, remove with a slotted spoon and drain on kitchen paper.
Coat each fritter with sugar and serve at once.

COQUES DE TORRÓ

Coca de turrón   Marzipan

A typical Majorcan sweetmeat available only at Christmas from
the bakers or grocers. The circular white wafers which enclose
the marzipan are on sale in bakers' and some grocers' shops just
before Christmas.

400 g (12 oz) ground
   almonds
400 g (12 oz) brown sugar
grated zest of 1 lemon

2 white wafers (*hostias*)
   or cut your own circular
   shapes from rice paper
   about 20 cm in
   diameter.

Mix the almonds, sugar and lemon zest together. Sandwich
between the two wafers and leave for one or two days before
serving, cut into wedges.

AMARGOS

Amargos   Almond balls

A traditional Christmas sweetmeat.

250 g (9 oz) ground almonds	grated zest of one lemon
100 g (3 ½ fl oz) sugar	½ tbsp flour
½ tsp ground cinnamon	1 egg

Mix all the ingredients together. The mixture should be dry and look like breadcrumbs, but be sticky enough to form small balls the size of walnuts when squeezed into shape in the hand. If the mixture will not hold, add one egg yolk; but it must be fairly dry or the almond balls will collapse in the oven.

Grease and flour a baking tray and place the balls on top and bake at 150°C (290°F, gas mark 1) for 15 minutes, keeping a careful eye on the balls to see they do not burn — which they do quite easily.

GATO

Tarta de almendras   Almond cake

A very moist cake that keeps well for a few days. It is the cake for special *fiestas,* including Christmas, and makes a good pudding when served with Majorcan ice cream. One of the best cake shops on the island is Casa Pomar in calle Plaza, 20, Campos, with a small branch in calle Antonio Marqúes Marqúes, 30, Palma. Their speciality is *gato* and they reckon to sell about 50,000 kilos of it a year. It is made with almonds, sugar, eggs, cinnamon and grated lemon peel for, says Juan Riutort, one of the owners: 'An authentic *gato* is not made with flour.'

Nevertheless, I have been shown how to make *gato* by an elderly Majorcan lady living in Puerto de Andraitx who always puts a small amount of flour into the *gato* she makes every Christmas. So, I give two versions: one with and one without flour.

These cakes are traditionally baked in deep cake tins with

slightly inward-sloping sides. The quantities given here require the smallest size tin, 6½ cm (2½") deep by 25 cm (10") wide, but an ordinary solid-bottomed cake tin will do just as well.

Version 1

250 g (9 oz) ground
  almonds
250 g (9 oz) sugar

6 eggs
1 tbsp flour

Beat the sugar and the egg yolks for twenty minutes by hand or for a few minutes with an electric mixer until light and creamy. Stir in the flour and almonds and beat the egg whites until they stand in peaks. Beat into the cake mixture until well incorporated and very creamy. Grease the cake tin and flour it well. Pour in the mixture and bake at 180°C (355°F, gas mark 4) for one hour. Check the cake, which is not harmed by opening the oven door for a few minutes, by inserting a skewer in the centre. If it comes out clean, remove the cake, but if not, leave it in the oven for another 5 or 10 minutes. Cool in the tin before turning out and sprinkle liberally with icing sugar.

Version 2

300 g (11 oz) ground
  almonds
300 g (11 oz) sugar
7 eggs

1 tsp ground cinnamon
the finely grated zest of
  1 lemon

Beat the egg yolks and sugar for 20 minutes by hand or for a few minutes with an electric mixer until light and creamy. Stir in the almonds, lemon zest and cinnamon. Now beat the egg whites until they stand in peaks. Beat into the cake mixture until well incorporated and very creamy. Follow the previous recipe for baking and serving.

BESCUITS

Bizcochos o Cuartos de Mallorca   Fatless sponge cakes

I was once told that sponge cake was introduced to England by Philip of Spain when he married Mary Tudor, the idea being that the word 'sponge' was a corruption of 'Spanish'. However, this seems to be a myth; sponge, as one would expect, comes from the Greek and Latin words meaning sponge.

This fatless sponge is common to bakeries throughout Majorca and can be served plain, just sprinkled with icing sugar, or filled with cream, confectioner's custard or jam. This recipe comes from Patisseria Bisyanea of calle Juan XXIII, 92, Puerto de Pollensa.

10 egg yolks   }   beaten together until
150 g (5 oz) sugar   }   creamy and thick

10 egg whites, stiffly beaten until standing in peaks
150 g (5 oz) sugar

200 g (7 oz) cornflour   }   sieved
75 g (2½ oz) flour   }   together

Mix the egg yolk mixture with the beaten egg whites, folding the egg whites in carefully until well incorporated, and adding the sugar at the same time. Slowly and carefully fold in the sifted flour. Grease and flour a cake tin about 6-7 cm (2½ ") deep and 25 cm (10") wide and pour in the mixture. Bake at 180°C (355°F, gas mark 4) for 30-40 minutes.

Let the cake cool in the tin slightly before turning it out and either sprinkling it with icing sugar or splitting it and filling with jam and cream.

The mixture can also be poured into metal or paper cake cups to make individual sponge cakes. These would take about 15 minutes at the same temperature in the oven.

ROBIOLS

Robioles   Sweet pastries

Robioles are especially popular at Easter, when they are filled with angel's hair jam. At other times they may have any of three fillings: confectioner's custard; *requeson,* a sweetened cream cheese; or, again, angel's hair jam.

75 g (2½ oz) lard	50 g (2 oz) sugar
330 g (12 oz) flour	1 egg yolk
90 ml (3½ fl oz) olive oil	juice of 1 orange

Rub the lard into the flour and then stir in the oil. Add the sugar, mixing it in well. Beat the egg yolk with the orange juice and blend that in to form a dough. If it seems to be a little on the dry side, stir in some water. Roll it out on a floured board and cut it into 12 cm (5″) rounds.

Put a heaped teaspoon of filling, either angel's hair jam (p 211), confectioner's custard (p 212) or *requeson,* cream cheese sweetened to taste with sugar and grated lemon peel, then moisten the edges and close in a half-moon shape. Bake in a medium oven at 180°C (355°F, gas mark 4) for 25-30 minutes. To serve, dust with icing sugar and serve warm or cold. You will find that you have about 12 *robiols.*

ROBIOLS FRITS

Robioles fritos   Fried sweet pastries

This recipe will produce 10 to 12 of the pastries.

100 g (3 oz) lard	confectioner's custard
3 eggs, beaten	(p 212) or angel's
200-250 g (7-9 oz) flour	hair jam (p 211)
olive oil for frying	

Soften the lard and mix it with the beaten eggs — it will not blend completely. Add the flour in small quantities until a stiff dough has formed; it is difficult to give the exact amount, but you will use at least 200 g (7 oz).

Roll out the dough and cut out rounds of 10 cm (4"). Put confectioner's custard on angel's hair jam in the centre, fold over in a half-moon shape and seal the edges well. Deep fry until golden on both sides in hot olive oil.

Serve hot with clear honey.

CABEY D'ANGEL

Cabello de angel   Angel's hair jam

Angel's hair jam, made from pumpkins, is easily obtainable in Majorca around Easter, when it is customary to make cakes such as *robiols* (see previous page) which contain it. It is sold loose and by the kilo. At other times it is rather difficult to come by, though it is a common filling for many pastries on sale in bakers' shops and cake shops all year round.

Cut a small pumpkin in half and scoop out the seeds from the centre of each half. Put the halves in a large saucepan, cover with cold water, and boil for about half an hour. Leave them in the water until they are cool enough to handle, then drain them and peel off the thick skin.

Now drain and weigh the pumpkin flesh. Return it to the saucepan with an equal weight of sugar and half the volume (of the pumpkin alone, not of the mixture) of water. Bring this to the boil and boil for 15 minutes, stirring. Leave it in the saucepan for 24 hours, then boil for another 15 minutes, stirring. If the mixture seems too dry and likely to burn, add a little more water.

Leave overnight again, and once more boil for 15 minutes next day. The pumpkin should by now be a rich brown colour. Remove it from the heat and let it cool, then either store it in sealed glass jars like other jams or do as Majorcans do, which is just to keep it in the refrigerator until it has been used.

CREMA

Crema   Confectioner's custard

100 g (3 oz) sugar	3 egg yolks
15 g (½ oz) cornflour	grated zest of 1 small lemon
¼ litre (9 fl oz) milk	½ tsp cinnamon

Mix the sugar and cornflour together, and dissolve the mixture in a little of the milk. Beat in the egg yolks and add the remaining milk, lemon zest and cinnamon. Pour the mixture into a saucepan, set it on a low heat and bring it to the boil, stirring continuously. It will thicken as it comes to the boil.

Remove from the heat and leave to cool. The *crema* is used as a filling for various pastries, in much the same way as its French equivalent, *crème patissière*.

GREIXONERA DE BROSSAT

Postre de requeson   Cheesecake

Requeson is a cream cheese often served for dessert in Majorca, usually sweetened with honey, lemon peel and cinnamon. It is also used as a filling for various pastries, again sweetened to taste with sugar or honey.

The *requeson* cheesecake varies significantly from village to village. The older recipes produce very sweet cheesecakes; the original version of the one I give here called for twice as much sugar — far too much for modern tastes.

500 g (1 lb) *requeson*	100 g (3½ oz) sugar
125 ml (4 fl oz) milk	1 level tsp ground cinnamon
grated zest of 1 lemon	6 eggs, well beaten

Mix all the ingredients together and place the mixture in a well-oiled *greixonera* (earthenware dish). Bake at 180°C (355°F, gas mark 4) for half an hour. Allow to cool before serving.

MEMBRILLO

Membrillo   Quince paste

Quinces were popular in England in medieval times, but have now become comparatively rare; they are not grown commercially. In Majorca they are cheap and plentiful, in late summer and the autumn; a mis-shapen, ugly fruit, which looks like a cross between an apple and a pear.

All over Spain they make a quince paste to be eaten with cheese or bread. This is very popular in Majorca. Locally made quince paste appears in the shops in the autumn and the big slabs of richly-coloured jelly are well worth seeking out. Or you can make your own as follows.

Wash 3 or 4 quinces and cut them up roughly without peeling or coring the fruit. Put them in a heavy-bottomed saucepan containing water about 3 cm (1") deep. Cover the pan and simmer until the fruit is soft. Sieve it or pass it through a vegetable mill and weigh the resulting pulp.

Put the pulp with an equal weight of sugar into the cleaned saucepan. Bring to the boil and simmer (it will spit somewhat) for about 25 minutes, just to the point where it first starts to pull away from the sides of the saucepan. Then pour the paste into ungreased foil tray containers or into ice cube trays and leave it to cool and set. Stored in the refrigerator, sealed in foil, it keeps for some months.

FRUITES SEQUES

Frutos secos   Dried fruit and nuts

Nuts and dried fruit are served as they are for dessert in Majorca. One popular way of ending a meal is to serve a fresh banana with a handful of lightly toasted almonds.

Amongst the many sweetmeats made with dried fruits, one that was traditionally only made for Christmas is now more often available. It is a fig bread made with minced dried figs, anise and fennel and moulded into small cone-shaped loaves before being slightly baked in the oven on a bed of lemon leaves.

GELATS

Helados   Ices

It was probably the Moors who introduced to Majorca the method of collecting snow from the mountain tops in winter and packing it into snow-houses to form ice for use in the summer months. Snow-houses (*casas de nieve*) were deep, stone-walled pits dug above the snowline and filled with snow by gangs of men who would tread and pack the snow down hard. The pits were then covered over with a good thick layer of twigs, and the ice would remain frozen solid until the arrival of warmer weather. One man would stay up there to look after the ice, for example renewing the covering on the pits from time to time.

In summer, and always at night, blocks of ice weighing as much as 50 kilos would be cut out and loaded onto mules to be transported down to the towns and villages to make ice creams and iced drinks. It was not until the Twenties that the first ice-making factories opened on the island, and some of these snow houses were in operation until 1925.

Some of the best ice cream in Majorca is that made by C'an Juan de s'Aigo, situated, for the last ten years, at number 10, calle Sans, in Palma. The business was founded in 1700, when the original owner transported ice from the snow-houses of Puig Mayor and stored it in his cellar. He used it to chill the pure water, flavoured with a few drops of lemon juice, which he sold in the summer months. (The name Ca'n Juan de s'Aigo is Majorcan for the House of John of the Water). From this stemmed a limited production of ice creams. Almond, hazelnut, vanilla and chocolate ices, available all year round, plus the seasonal strawberry and apricot ones are the best known of these.

GELAT D'AMETILLA

Helado de almendra   Almond ice cream

Apart from Ca'n Juan de s'Aigo there are quite a few ice cream shops dotted about the island making ice cream on the premises. Ca'n Nero of Andraitx is one such. Bars in the vicinity of these shops will often display signs during the summer advertising the fact that they serve the locally produced ice cream.

The very best of all the Majorcan ice creams is the almond ice cream. Occasionally Majorcan restaurants offer one of the few truly Majorcan puddings to be seen on restaurant menus — *gato* (p 207) — with the accompaniment of almond ice cream. If you think of having this, make sure that the ice cream is home-made; manufactured almond ice cream is nowhere near as good.

The real Majorcan almond 'ice cream' resembles a water ice. This recipe comes from Heladeria Ca'n Miquel, number 6 in calle Jaime III, Palma.

250 g (9 oz) blanched almonds, finely ground	1 litre (36 fl oz) water finely grated zest of one lemon
300 g (10 oz) sugar	1 small stick cinnamon

Place all the ingredients together in a saucepan and put this on a very low heat. Bring it slowly to the boil, stirring frequently. As soon as the mixture boils, remove the pan from the heat and leave to cool. Remove the cinnamon stick and either pour the liquid into a machine for making ice cream or freeze it in the freezer compartment of the refrigerator, stirring from time to time as it is setting.

215

GRANISSATS

Granizados   Iced drinks

Of Moorish origin, *granizado* is a version of the Middle Eastern sorbet, which became the Italian *granita:* but in Majorca it is served as a thick, icy drink usually made from the juice of a citrus fruit. It is available at most ice cream parlours and some bars during the summer months.

GRANISSAT DE LLIMONA

Granizado de limon   Iced lemon drink

4 medium lemons   250 g (9 oz) sugar
grated zest from 1 lemon   ¾ litre (27 fl oz) water

Boil the water, sugar and grated lemon zest together for a few minutes, stirring until the sugar is dissolved. Leave to cool and strain the liquid. Stir in the unstrained juice of the lemons.

Pour this mixture into a mould and freeze it in the freezing compartment of the refrigerator. As the ice freezes beat it with a fork to reduce the size of the ice crystals. Repeat a few times at half hourly intervals. Do not let it set solid, but hold it in the refrigerator for half an hour before serving it in tall glasses as a thick, icy drink full of ice crystals.

GRANISSAT DE TARONJA

Granizado de naranja   Iced orange drink

6 oranges   ¾ litre (27 fl oz) water
250 g (9 oz) sugar

Boil the water and sugar together for few minutes, stirring all the time until the sugar is dissolved. Leave to cool and add the unstrained juice of the oranges. Freeze and serve in the same way as the lemon *granizado* above.

ORXATA D'AMETILLA

Horchata de almendras   Almond milk

This is an unusual sweet iced drink made from almonds and available only in the Balearic Islands and on the Valencian coast, although a similar almond drink is prepared in the Middle East.

Horchata de chufa, a similar drink made from tiger nuts, is more common throughout Spain, in fact it is frequently sold in milk bottles in the milk section of supermarkets (which can be confusing as all *horchatas* are milky coloured drinks).

You can buy a condensed form of the almond milk given here to which you just add chilled water, but I find this commercial preparation too sweet.

250 g (9 oz) freshly ground almonds	2 tbsp sugar, or to taste
	1 small stick cinnamon
1 litre (36 fl oz) water	rind of 1 lemon

Soak the almonds in the water overnight. The resulting liquid will be white and fragrant. Sieve this almond milk into a saucepan, pressing down on the almonds to extract as much of the liquid as possible. Add the sugar, cinnamon and lemon peel and bring very slowly to the boil. Simmer for a few minutes, stirring frequently, then remove from the heat and leave to cool before removing the cinnamon stick and the lemon peel.

Serve chilled as a refreshing summer drink.

Bibliography

AGULLÓ I VIDAL, FERRAN, *Llibre de la Cuina Catalana* (2nd edn, of 1933), facsimile reprint (ed Llorens Torrado), Alta Fulla, Barcelona, 1978.

ASSOCIACIÓ EMPRESARIAL DE RESTAURACIÓ DE MALLORCA, recipes from La Mostra de la Cuina Mallorquina 1985 and 1986.

ANDREWS, COLMAN, *Catalan Cuisine*, Atheneum, New York, 1988.

BERARD, GEROMINO DE, *Viaje a las Villas de Mallorca 1789*, Ajuntament de Palma, 1983.

BIDWELL, C T, *Balearic Islands*, London, 1876.

BOYD, MARY STUART, *Fortunate Isles*, London, 1911.

CALERA, ANA MARIA, *Cocina Balear*, Editorial Everest SA, Léon, 1983.

CARR, SIR JOHN, *Descriptive Travels in the Southern and Eastern Parts of Spain and the Balearic Islands*, London, 1811.

CRESPI GREEN, VALERI, *Landscape of Mallorca*, Sunflower Books, London, 1984.

DAVIDSON, ALAN, *Mediterranean Seafood*, expanded and revised edn, Penguin Books, London, 1987.

FISCHER, DR WALTER and M SCHNEIDER (eds), *FAO Species Identification Sheets for the Mediterranean and Black Sea* (volume II, Vertebrates) Rome, 1987.

FORD, RICHARD, *Gatherings from Spain*, London 1846, reprinted by Dent in Everyman's Library from 1906 onwards.

GRAY, PATIENCE, *Honey from a Weed*, Prospect Books, London, 1986.

GREWE, RUDOLPH, 'Catalan Cuisine, in an Historical Perspective' in *National and Regional Styles of Cookery*, Oxford Symposium Documents, 1981.

JUAN DE CORRAL, CATY, *Cocina Balear: Las Cuatro Estaciones*, Edita: Caja de Baleares.

La Cuyna Mallorquina (1934), facsimile reprint, Palma Edicions, 1982.

218

MACAULEY, ROSE, *Crewe Train,* Collins, London, 1926.

MACMIADHACHÁIN, ANNA, *Spanish Regional Cookery,* Penguin Books, London, 1976.

MAJORCAN NEWSPAPERS, *Ultima Hora, Diario de Mallorca* and *Majorcan Daily Bulletin.*

MARCH, LOURDES, *El Libro de la Paella y de los Arroces,* Alianza Editorial, Madrid, 1985.

MARCH, LOURDES, *La Cocina Mediterránea,* Alianza Editorial, Madrid, 1988.

MATEU, JAUME, *Llibre de Gelats i Quemuyars,* Luis Ripoll, 1978.

POMÉS, LEOPOLD, *Teoria i Practica del Pa amb Tomàquet,* Tusquets Editors, Barcelona, 1985.

PPC (Petits Propos Culinaires, an English-language journal on food history), issues 1-33, Prospect Books, London, 1979-89.

RIPOLL, LUIS, *Llibre de Vins, Licors i per Necessari,* Colleccion Siurell, 1974.

RIPOLL, LUIS, *Cocina de la Baleares,* Colleccion Siurell, 1984.

RIPOLL, LUIS (ed) *Libro de Recetas de Ca'n Esteva: Dulces, Pastas, Confituras, Turrones* (1862), Palma de Mallorca, 1986.

RODEN, CLAUDIA, *A Book of Middle Eastern Food,* Nelson, London, 1968, and in the Penguin series since 1970.

SAND, GEORGE, *Winter in Majorca,* (trs) Robert Graves, Cassell, London, 1956.

SHEPPARD, LADY, *Mediterranean Island,* London, 1949.

THURSTON, HAZEL, *The Travellers Guide to the Balearics: Majorca, Minorca, Ibiza and Formentera,* The Leisure Circle, Wembley, Middlesex, 1979.

VIDAL, COLOMA ABRINAS, *Cocina Selecta Mallorquina,* decima-quinta edición, 1982.

Vinos de Espana 1985/6 (Guia práctica para amantes y profes-sionales de los Club de Gourmets), Grupo Editorial, Madrid, 1985.

WHELPTON, ERIC, *The Balearics,* London, 1952.

WOLFERT, PAULA, *Good Food from Morocco,* John Murray, London, 1989.

WOOD, CHARLES W, *Letters from Majorca,* London, 1888.

Indexes

There are three indexes: Mallorquin; Castilian Spanish; and English. Each covers all the recipe titles, plus the ingredients described in the first part of the book.

MALLORQUIN

Index

CASTILIAN

Index

ENGLISH